Politics, Murder, and Love
in Stalin's Kremlin

The Story of Nikolai Bukharin and Anna Larina

Politics, Murder, and Love in Stalin's Kremlin

The Story of Nikolai Bukharin and Anna Larina

Paul R. Gregory

HOOVER INSTITUTION PRESS
Stanford University   *Stanford, California*

Hoover Institution Press Publication No. 579

Hoover Institution at Leland Stanford Junior University,
Stanford, California, 94305-6010

First printing 2010
16   15   14   13   12   11   10   9   8   7   6   5   4   3   2   1

Manufactured in the United States of America

The paper used in this publication meets the minimum
Requirements of the American National Standard for
Information Sciences—Permanence of Paper for Printed
Library Materials, ANSI/NISO Z39.48-1992. ♾

Cataloging-in-Publication Data is available from the Library of Congress

ISBN-13: 978-0-8179-1034-1   (cloth : alk. paper)
ISBN-13: 978-0-8179-1035-8   (paperback : alk. paper)
ISBN-13: 978-0-8179-1036-5   (e-book version)

Contents

Foreword

by Robert Conquest

Paul Gregory has a great record of investigating the realities of the former Soviet regime. He has helped restore truths long hidden in murky, dusty files, into whose still incompletely explored riches he has been one of the most helpful investigators. In a number of books that have been welcomed and praised in Russia as well as in the academic West, Gregory has added much in the way of economic and organizational understanding. If there are still details to be filled in, and some to be corrected, that is always true of serious historical research. His present book, however, is not in this category. It is, as he says, for the general reader.

There is a whole literature on the recovery of the realities of an intellectually as well as physically repressive political and social order. And within this genre lie many human tragedies. What Gregory has done here is to give that background as the locus of personal dramas centered on the acts and motivations of three of the most revealing figures in the frightful Soviet maelstrom (Bukharin, his wife Anna, and Stalin), in a series of vignettes in which the dramatis personae meet in a long struggle for two of them merely to survive—a struggle the Bukharins lost. Coming from the party elite, they do not so much typify as illustrate the already raging mass terror of unpolitical, non-intellectual victims, whom they then joined.

Just as Gregory has avoided the formality of the lecture hall, so has he actively rejected dry formalism. His scenes are centered on the emotional drama, on the acts and feelings of the protagonists.

The political infighting stands out in the context of character and feeling—more effectively so than in pure fiction.

Many academic readers are professionally concerned with the whole fearful ambience of Stalinism. Here is what many others will find readable: a story told to show the horrors of fate, of personal mistreatment and suffering by real people. Their thoughts and feelings were often ill-suited to the crushing environment and are often most visible in the vivid context of Gregory's feuilletons, which come together as tragedy.

At this level, the book works as a romance and even as a thriller. Thus, it is suitable for a broad, non-specialist audience, which will be instructed as well as entertained.

Preface

THIS BOOK TELLS THE TRAGEDY of one death and one ruined life—that of Stalin's most prominent victims—Nikolai Bukharin and his wife, Anna Larina. Stories such as theirs may offer more insights than general accounts of Stalin's purges. Their saga contains all the elements of high drama: love and devotion interspersed with intrigue, betrayal, hope, weakness, friendship, naïveté, endurance, optimism, bitterness, and ultimate tragedy.

Nikolai Bukharin was a founding father of the new Bolshevik state at the age of twenty-nine. Well educated and charming, he became an intimate of the exiled Lenin, who later dubbed him "the favorite of the party." A rising star, Bukharin was the editor of *Pravda*, and he joined the elite Politburo following Lenin's death. After forming an alliance with Stalin to remove Leon Trotsky from power, Bukharin crossed swords with Stalin over their differing visions of the world's first socialist state.

Anna Larina was the daughter of a high Bolshevik official, one of Bukharin's closest friends. She was three years old at the founding of the Bolshevik state. They married seventeen years later, on her twentieth birthday. Following Bolshevik custom, there was no formal wedding. Anna simply moved into Nikolai's Kremlin apartment, and they were scarcely apart until his arrest in 1937. Theirs was a remarkably close relationship based on friendship and then love.

The story of Nikolai Bukharin and Anna Larina begins with the optimism of the socialist revolution, but turns into a dark tale of foreboding and then terror—as the game changes from political struggle to physical survival. Theirs is also a tale of courage and cowardice, strength and weakness, misplaced idealism, missed opportunities, bungling, and, above all, love.

Stalin was purported to have quipped that "one death is a tragedy; a thousand is a statistic."[1] Nikolai Bukharin was only one of the millions of the dictator's victims. Most were ordinary people, whereas Nikolai and Anna belonged to the Bolshevik elite. But their story takes us from the "statistic" to the "tragedy," and provides a more enduring understanding of Stalin and Stalinism than the tally of the millions he ordered killed.

Bukharin's tale also sounds a cautionary note for those sympathetic to benevolent dictatorships as a way of escaping national poverty. The dictator can turn out to be a Stalin instead of a Bukharin—a Saddam Hussein or Robert Mugabe instead of Singapore's Lee Kuan Yew. Of the possible successors to Lenin, Bukharin most clearly spelled out a vision, which today would be called "socialism with a human face." His loss suggests that Stalin's victory was predetermined by factors deeply embedded in the Bolshevik revolution. Bukharin proved helpless against a ruthless competitor who thirsted for absolute power.

PAUL GREGORY
Houston and Palo Alto, December 2009

Acknowledgments

THIS BOOK TELLS THE TALE of Nikolai Bukharin and Anna Larina's losing battle with Stalin. *Politics, Murder, and Love in Stalin's Kremlin* grew out of conversations with John Raisian, director of the Hoover Institution, and Richard Sousa, deputy director and director of library and archives. They encouraged me to use my explorations of the Hoover Archives to write a book that would appeal to both professional and general readers. After reading the transcript of Nikolai Bukharin's crucifixion before the central committee plenum of February 1937, I knew I had found an epic tale that would draw readers into the dark labyrinth that was Stalin's Russia.

The professionals of the Hoover Archives and Hoover Press— Linda Bernard, Carol Leadenham, Anatol Shmelev, Lora Soroka, and David Sun (archives), Marshall Blanchard, Jennifer Navarrette, Jennifer Presley, and Eryn Witcher (press and publicity)—helped me at each step. A number of scholars generously read and commented on various drafts, allowing me to avoid mistakes and refine my interpretations. In particular, I would like to thank Anne Appelbaum, Robert Gellately, Mark Harrison, Steven Kotkin, Hiroyaki Kuromiya, Priscilla McMillan, Norman Naimark, Bert Patenaude, David Shearer, Robert Service and Amir Weiner. A special note of thanks goes to Robert Conquest, who encouraged me with great enthusiasm and whose foreword captures the essence of the book. I must single out Stephen Cohen, whose landmark biography of Nikolai Bukharin reintroduced him to the historical record and whose efforts on behalf of Bukharin studies have been untiring. He provided me with invaluable comments and intellectual challenges, which sharpened my presentation. The photograph of Anna Larina, which graces the cover, is from his private collection.

It is not the job of colleagues to locate errors and misinterpretations. They remain fully my responsibility. The fact that I recognize their generous comments in no way signifies their endorsement.

The editorial guidance of Roger Williams elicited major improvements throughout the text. Natalia Reshetova provided invaluable research assistance. Christian Teichman of Humboldt University and Martin Kroeger of the Archive of the German Foreign Office provided valuable information on Bukharin records in Germany.

Given that this book targets a general audience, I must thank the lay readers who read and commented on various drafts. They include Anne Harrison, Grover Liese, Allen Lock, Thomas Mayor, John Michalski, Anastas Pass, Walton Shim, Henry and Janet Steele, and Carey West.

Introduction

THE BOLSHEVIK REVOLUTION unexpectedly brought to power a disparate collection of idealists, misfits, fanatics, intellectuals, scoundrels, opportunists, and some outright criminals and thugs. Nikolai Bukharin belonged in the idealist and intellectual categories. Stalin began as a thug—the organizer of bank robberies and murders in his native Georgia.[2] As underground revolutionaries who had spent years on the run or in exile, the Bolsheviks now had to decide, in Lenin's earlier words, "what is to be done." The answer was a party dictatorship, which would decide the interests of workers and peasants, whether they liked it or not. In candid conversations, Bolshevik leaders described peasants as greedy ("They would steal from St. Peter if they could")[3] and workers as lazy and shiftless—scarcely appropriate sentiments for the leaders of the first "worker-peasant state."

From the beginning, there was no pretense of democracy. The 1918 Red Terror Decree ordered the "arrest of all prominent Mensheviks and rightist Socialist Revolutionaries."[4] Lenin's first extraordinary decree shut down the independent press. His second called for the arrest of "non-Soviet" authors, scientists, and intellectuals.[5] The Communist Party was henceforth to dictate the truth; the press and sanctioned "Soviet" intellectuals were to confirm it.[6] Thereafter, the ensuing power struggle centered on who was to define that truth and what would happen to those who disagreed.

Vladimir Il'ich Lenin was the consensual leader who could be challenged by other top party officials on key issues. He and the tempestuous Bukharin clashed bitterly over the Brest-Litovsk Treaty that ended the war with Germany, but their friendship survived.[7] Not only did Lenin officially head the government, as the head of the Council of People's Commissars, he also chaired meetings of the Politburo, which he and other Bolshevik founders recognized as the supreme authority.[8] Stalin was the general secretary of the party's Central Committee. As such, he began to consolidate control over party business and appointments. The party grew rapidly. It numbered two hundred thousand at the time of the October Revolution. The Seventeenth Congress of Victors, which convened in January 1934 to celebrate Stalin's triumphs, was attended by two thousand delegates representing nearly three million party members.[9] As Nikita Khrushchev revealed twenty-two years later, to a shocked Twentieth Party Congress, almost half of these delegates perished shortly thereafter in Stalin's Great Terror.

The Russian civil war, which erupted in early 1918, was a struggle for survival, with the Bolsheviks battling units loyal to the Czar as well as Polish, Cossack, and Western forces. Lenin dispatched his Politburo colleagues, including Stalin, to the front. Casualties were high on the battlefield and behind the lines, as both sides committed horrendous atrocities. Lenin's "armed sword" was the feared Cheka secret police led by Feliks Dzerzhinskii, whose officers tortured opponents, drowned prisoners by the boatload, and dispatched others with casual, summary executions. Trotsky's frenetic heroics, as the architect and creator of the Red Army, made him the most charismatic of the founding fathers. By the end of 1920, the Bolshevik victory appeared assured.

In March 1921, Lenin dismayed party hardliners, including Bukharin, by announcing the New Economic Policy to replace the teetering war economy. Peasants were again free to sell their grain, and private trade was allowed to flourish along with small-scale industry. Lenin's gamble succeeded. The economic recovery was rapid, but many Bolsheviks considered it a betrayal of the Communist cause.

After suffering a second stroke in December 1922, Lenin withdrew from active political life. He died on January 21, 1924.

Although he left a political testament counseling the "rude" Stalin's removal, the document named no successor, touching off a power struggle with a bloody end: of the nine members of the Politburo on the day of Lenin's death, only three died of natural causes. One of the three was Stalin himself. When the struggle began, however, few knew that it would literally be for life or death.

No Bolshevik leader wanted to succeed Lenin more fervently than did Stalin, who, according to his former secretary, "had only one passion, absolute and devouring: lust for power."[10] There were other candidates. Mikhail Tomskii had a base in the trade union movement, was quick on his feet, and possessed a sharp wit; but he suffered from depression and alcoholism. Grigory Zinovyev headed both the Leningrad party and the Communist International, known as the Comintern. Lev Kamenev was the de facto head of government during Lenin's incapacitation. Both, however, were Jewish in a country with a history of anti-Semitism.

The best known of the Bolshevik founders was another Jew, Leon Trotsky, the charismatic commissar of the Red Army. Lenin's testament characterized him as the "most capable" Bolshevik leader, and he was widely believed to be the most likely successor. But the aloof, vainglorious, and politically inept Trotsky relinquished command of the army with scarcely a fight in 1925. Henceforth, only his charismatic reputation and membership in the Politburo constituted real strengths among his dwindling political assets. In the end, Trotsky played the Lenin card too late (at a September 1927 Politburo meeting), only to be deftly brushed aside by Stalin.[11]

The Politburo members occupying the highest official positions were Aleksei Rykov, who replaced Lenin as chair of the Council of People's Commissars, and Stalin, who occupied the faceless position of general secretary of the Central Committee, shuffling paper while others supposedly did the real business of the party. Rykov controlled the levers of government; Stalin controlled the party machine in what would turn out to be an unfair match. Rykov was an efficient technocrat, despite his alcoholism, while Stalin's detractors perceived him as a plodder and dullard. A joke from Trotsky captured the prevailing perceptions of the two: "Trotsky dictates in his last will that, upon his death, his brain should be preserved in alcohol, with the instruction that the brain goes to Stalin and the alcohol to Rykov."[12]

Nikolai Bukharin was a contender with many handicaps. Aside from a following of students, he lacked an independent power base. He had not headed any organization of note, having spent the brutal civil war years in Moscow, largely spared the war's violence. His posts as editor of *Pravda* and as the party's socialist theoretician gave him power over words and ideas but not people.

In June 1924, a new competitor entered the ring when Mikhail Frunze was elected a candidate (non-voting) member of the Politburo. A strong personality with outstanding revolutionary and military credentials (the son of a peasant plus a civil war hero), Frunze had the weight of the army behind him—making him a potent rival to Stalin. Many were not surprised, therefore, when in October of the following year he died of chloroform poisoning during a botched stomach operation that had been arranged by Stalin in his capacity of general secretary. Belief was widespread that Stalin ordered Frunze's murder.[13]

Stalin's rivals underestimated his willingness to fight as underhandedly as necessary for as long as needed. The flaw his rivals thought would be fatal was Lenin's prescient deathbed advice to "think about a way of removing Stalin."[14]

Some of Lenin's highest praise was reserved for Iurii Piatakov, an industrial official, whom he called a "man of outstanding will and outstanding ability." Such an endorsement guaranteed that Stalin's hatred for Piatakov would be intense. (Stalin had him executed in 1937 after torture that left him, as Bukharin would later describe, a "toothless skeleton.")

Stalin attacked his opponents from the bastion of the Central Committee, using the "unlimited power" of which Lenin had warned. Stalin knew the names, records, and flaws of virtually all those in high office. Whenever a position was vacant, he had a ready candidate, and he packed the Central Committee with loyalists. Stalin was also a master of pork-barrel politics; his industrialization programs offered attractive projects to regional party bosses whom he wanted on his side. In addition, Stalin placed men loyal to him in rival strongholds, such as in Zinovyev's Leningrad committee, Bukharin's *Pravda*, and Tomskii's trade unions.[15] When the time came, his supporters, although in the minority, could make trouble for their bosses.

Friendship with Stalin proved no guarantee of immunity to his unending crusade for power; only two of his sixty-five regional party secretaries survived the purges of 1935–38. Stalin executed his childhood friend and daughter's godfather, Avel' Enukidze, on trumped-up charges, declaring him "a foreigner to us."[16] He bugged telephones and spent hours listening in on private conversations.[17] (He found transcripts of intimate conversations between Zinovyev and his wife amusing and shared them with others.)[18]

Stalin played disconcerting psychological games. He threatened the timid titular head of state, Mikhail Kalinin, for meeting with an accused enemy of the state. He also frightened the plodding war minister, Kliment Voroshilov, by charging him with plotting a military dictatorship.[19] When both turned unexpectedly against Bukharin, the latter surmised that "Stalin has some special hold on them."[20]

Stalin directed psychological warfare particularly at Bukharin. One day he would accuse Bukharin of plotting his assassination and the next day toast him: "Let us drink, comrades, to Nikolai Ivanovich [Bukharin] and let bygones be bygones."[21] At the November 7, 1936, Red Square festivities, some three months before his compatriot's arrest, Stalin sent an emissary to tell Bukharin that he was "not in the right place" and to join him and the rest of the top leadership on the roof of Lenin's mausoleum.[22]

Upon Lenin's death in January 1924, Stalin's immediate task was to block Trotsky. He formed a "troika," with Kamenev and Zinovyev, that dominated the Politburo in 1924–25 and removed Trotsky from his official positions. The three formed an effective team as they sat next to each other during Politburo meetings, exchanging notes and whispered conversations.[23]

Our story begins in 1926, as Stalin's troika with Kamenev and Zinovyev was falling apart, and Stalin was forming a new Politburo majority with Bukharin and his allies, Prime Minister Rykov and trade union leader Tomskii.

In 1926, Nikolai Bukharin was thirty-eight years old. His future wife, Anna Larina, was twelve.

CHAPTER 1

April 15, 1937:
A Plea from Prison

IT IS LATE NIGHT or early morning—the prisoner has little sense of time. He uses the night hours to work feverishly on his writing, following days filled with interrogations and negotiations. He repositions himself periodically to take advantage of the dim light from a single, naked bulb. His small cell is littered with books and papers that he has wheedled from his captors. Tonight he has put aside work on a semi-autobiographical novel to compose a letter to the person who controls his fate. He addresses the man warmly, assuring him that "there are no bad feelings despite [your] removing me from my surroundings and sending me here."

The prisoner, nearing his fiftieth birthday, is small in stature; a prominent mustache and goatee divert attention from a hairline that began receding in youth. His hair is gray, but small wisps of the original red color remain visible. Periodically, he paces his cell, then returns to his task.

His letter, addressed "Dear Koba," rambles, runs on at tedious length, and intersperses hysteria, anger, bitterness, and remorse with ambitious plans for the future. He describes his life in prison, writing as if to allay any concerns "Koba" might have that he is being mistreated. (He has ceased to go outside for exercise because he feels ashamed when other prisoners look at him.) The prison regime is strict: no feeding of the pigeons, no talking in the corridors, no noises in the cell, a light burning day and night. But it's also fair: the food is good, and even the young jailors treat him decently.

Parts of the letter appear bizarrely inappropriate: "In my lifetime, I have known intimately only four women." At the end, the prisoner makes his plea: "Settle me in a hut somewhere outside of Moscow, give me a new name, let two NKVD officers live in my home, allow me to live with my family, let me work for the common good with books and translations under a pseudonym, let me till the soil." The letter ends: "My heart is breaking that this is a Soviet prison and my grief and burden are without limit. Be healthy and happy." The signature read "N. Bukharin," and the date noted was April 15, 1937.[24]

Bukharin's "Dear Koba" was, of course, Joseph Stalin, the uncontested master of the Russian house. Following his usual pretense of giving his deputies a voice, Stalin wrote on the border of his transmittal letter: "Circulate!" and listed seven Politburo members as recipients. Their predictable reactions came back in a torrent: "The letter of a criminal"; "A criminal farce"; and "A typical Bukharin lie."

Stalin was thus again obliged to bend reluctantly to the "will of the party." Bukharin could not be freed; he would have to stand trial and receive his punishment. As Stalin had told him at the time of his arrest, "Friendship is friendship, but duty is duty."[25] Old pal Koba was simply doing that duty.

Nikolai Bukharin was the most prominent political prisoner ever held in the Internal Prison of the NKVD. Dubbed the "Golden Boy" of the revolution by none other than Vladimir Il'ich Lenin, Bukharin had nonetheless fallen from the apex of the party hierarchy. By odd and ironic coincidence, Lenin's praise was uttered in the presence of five-year-old Anna Larina, who fifteen years later would become Bukharin's wife.[26]

The praise and exalted stature were not surprising. Bukharin was widely regarded as a leading Marxist theorist, second only to Lenin. Among the best educated of the Bolshevik founding fathers, he organized student revolts at Moscow University at the age of sixteen and became a member of the Moscow Soviet in 1908, at the age of twenty. Arrested several times, he was sent to internal exile in Onega in 1910 for incendiary speeches and organizing worker protests.

From there, he fled abroad, attended courses in German universities, and became an associate of Lenin—also an exile living in Krakow and then Switzerland.

Bukharin traveled a rocky road: he was arrested and expelled from both Austria and Switzerland. In 1916, he entered the United States illegally and found work there as a correspondent for the Russian-language daily, *Novy Mir*. In New York, he met Trotsky, whose impression of Bukharin was not positive (a "medium through whom someone else's thoughts could be channeled").[27]

Nonetheless, Bukharin became a prominent figure. The author of numerous books and articles, fluent in French and German and widely traveled, he served as the editor of *Pravda* from the first days of the October Revolution. A man of great intellectual enthusiasm and curiosity, he attracted disciples to his "Bukharin school," later belittled by Stalin as Bukharin's "little school" *(shkolka)*. He read and composed poetry avidly, and his caricatures of Old Bolsheviks, doodled during Politburo meetings, remain classics.[28]

But Bukharin also had telling weaknesses. He was impulsive, sensitive, prone to hysteria under stress, incapable of political calculation, and a self-admitted terrible organizer. He cried over the loss of several hundred of his Moscow Bolshevik comrades during the October Revolution; he wept profusely at Lenin's deathbed; he required sedation from Anna's mother after witnessing at first hand collectivization in Ukraine.[29] These traits led to a reputation of weakness among other Bolshevik leaders. (In the words of a fellow Politburo member: "I fear Bukharin because he is a soft-hearted person.")[30]

In addition, Bukharin too often talked and wrote without thinking—unlike his nemesis Stalin, who (as his former secretary remarked) "spoke little in a land that spoke too much."[31] Off-the-cuff remarks and chance meetings would come back to haunt him with terrible consequences. His sensitivity and volubility were later used to create the impression of a person not to be taken seriously. His colleagues used the term "Little Bukharin" *(Bukharchik)* in private and public. Normally a term of endearment, Stalin used it to belittle him.

Bukharin was also known to change positions, the most prominent being his shift in the mid-twenties from radical "Left Communism" to advocacy of the "liberal" New Economic Policy. Lenin characterized him as "soft wax" on which "unprincipled persons can make an impression."[32]

During the civil war, Lenin kept the "soft" Bukharin in Moscow to manage *Pravda* and Bolshevik propaganda. He thus retained a "halo of innocence," "spinning brilliant words and ideas in Moscow" while other Bolshevik founders razed towns and villages, and ordered executions and torture at the front.[33] But he did not escape the violence of the civil war entirely: he was wounded in an anarchist bomb attack that claimed twelve lives in Moscow.[34]

After Lenin's death, Bukharin was fully ensconced in the inner sanctum of power. Popular with the party rank-and-file, he, unlike other top Bolsheviks, moved freely around Moscow without guards and was greeted enthusiastically by Muscovites, who recognized him on sight. Bukharin often seemed, as described by a noted British historian, a "gentle and lovable character of singular personal charm."[35]

Bukharin married three times. As one of his friends declared to Anna Larina shortly before their wedding in 1934, "A holy place does not stay empty long."[36] His first marriage was to his slightly older first cousin, Nadezhda Lukina, before the revolution. The union proved childless and fell apart in the early 1920s, as her health deteriorated. Nadezhda took the breakup badly. In Bukharin's words: "She almost lost her mind. Lenin had to order her to go abroad."[37] Nadezhda nonetheless remained devoted to her former husband.

Bukharin became acquainted with his second wife, Esfir' Gurvich, in 1921, during a game of *gorodki* on the lawn of Lenin's suburban estate. Esfir' was an economist who also had a degree in architecture. Throughout their marriage, she lived in a separate apartment, not in the Kremlin. Esfir' and Stalin's wife, Nadezhda Allilueva, were close friends, and their daughters—both named Svetlana—were constant companions at Stalin's dacha. According to rumors, Stalin drove Gurvich and Bukharin apart in 1928 because she knew too much about Stalin's private life.[38]

Nikolai Bukharin remained committed to the ideal of a socialist state throughout his life. He continued to write voluminously on socialist theory, unwittingly providing Stalin with ammunition to accuse him of socialist heresy. His last instruction to his wife was to raise their infant son as a good Bolshevik "without fail." He had great faith in the eventual victory of socialism.

CHAPTER 2

March 15, 1938:
A Husband Executed

WORD OF NIKOLAI BUKHARIN'S execution came to his twenty-four-year-old spouse, Anna Larina, in the Tomsk camp for wives of "traitors of the fatherland." The warden clambered to the upper bed boards, opposite Anna, and read aloud to the hundred or so prisoners the newspaper account of the closing session of the third of Stalin's Show Trials. As she read, she glanced at Larina so she could report her reactions.

The charges against Bukharin included plotting with German fascists, organizing uprisings, participating in a plan to assassinate Lenin, attempting to murder Stalin, and actually murdering prominent Soviet officials, including Leningrad Party boss Sergei Kirov and writer Maksim Gorky. One of the more unbelievable charges was the attempted poisoning of NKVD head Nikolai Ezhov. Bukharin and all twenty other defendants entered guilty pleas. His sentence—death by firing squad—was carried out two days later.

To avoid the stares of the warden and others, and to hide profuse bleeding from her nose, Larina pulled the bed sheets over her head. The warden broke off her reading and rudely ordered the newly created widow to wash the floor of the corridor. Another prisoner mercifully volunteered in her place.

As the prison official read on, Larina had doubts that the man in the dock was really her husband, Nikolai Ivanovich Bukharin, and not some stand-in. If he had made such admissions to her in private, she would have considered him insane. But as far as Anna

was concerned, Nikolai was at that point already a dead man—
and had been one since the fateful day of his arrest in February
1937. Awareness that his suffering had ended brought a certain re-
lief. She only hoped that he would leave life proudly, declaring his
innocence.[39]

Larina was one of the few women in the Tomsk camp whose husband had undergone a public trial. Most of them, knowing nothing
of the fates of their husbands, continued to hope. The wife of a
Ukrainian party worker came up to her and said, reproachfully:
"Why are you moping? History will vindicate your husband. No
one will know about ours."[40]

The next morning, the warden confiscated Anna's only photograph of Iura, her eleven-month-old "Bukharinist" baby, ordered her
to pack, and sent her off to the next camp. She was shuttled among
camps until 1945, and even after her release, she had to remain in
exile for another decade.

Anna Larina was the stepdaughter of a high Bolshevik official, an
intimate of Lenin, Iurii Larin. He married Anna's aunt, who raised
her following her mother's death, a year after the girl was born.
Iurii Larin took part in the October Revolution as a leader of the
Petrograd Soviet. Hard-working and diligent, despite a birth defect
that left him partially lame, he occupied leading state positions as
Lenin assigned him to manage affairs of state. Many of Lenin's de-
crees were drafted by Larin.

Anna grew up in her father's apartment in the Metropole Hotel,
a stone's throw from the Kremlin. Among Larin's frequent visitors
were Lenin, Stalin, and other leading state and party figures, including a man twenty-six years Anna's senior, Nikolai Bukharin—short,
red haired, blue eyed, with a mustache and beard. He had known
"Larochka" since her fourth year, was her favorite among the visitors, and now lived in the flat below hers.

Bukharin taught the young girl to swim and to climb the mountains at the age of nine, while she vacationed in Sochi. She was disappointed that he usually came to see her father, not her. An only
child, she was delighted when in his company.

The Larins lived a simple life. Their Metropole apartment was cramped. Anna's stepmother/aunt had to watch the family budget carefully. Anna walked to school and rode public transportation. The family did have a dacha close to Moscow, and she spent summer vacations in the Crimea or Sochi with her family. Like her classmates, Anna joined the Communist Youth Organization. As a child of professional revolutionaries who was also close to Nikolai Bukharin, she developed an early interest in politics.

Little did her father suspect that she was clandestinely reading top-secret party documents taken from his desk. As a fourteen-year-old, she read the secret transcripts describing Bukharin's political defeat at the hands of Stalin. On her next visit to his apartment, she burst out in tears before the despondent older man.[41]

As Anna's beauty blossomed, Nikolai Bukharin's intentions changed from family friend to hesitant suitor. After his defeat, Bukharin retreated to the Crimea to recover from a lung infection. There the depressed Bukharin began his courtship by asking the sixteen-year-old Anna "if she would be able to love a leper."[42]

After an intermittent off-and-on courtship, Anna and Nikolai became husband and wife on Anna's twentieth birthday. In a twist of fate, the Kremlin apartment they occupied had belonged to Stalin, who exchanged it with Bukharin after the suicide of Stalin's wife, Nadezhda. (A congratulatory call from a drunken Stalin interrupted their wedding night.) The couple's son, Iura, was born in 1936.

Although Bukharin's political fortunes appeared to be improving at the time of their marriage—he was named editor of *Izvestiia* in 1934—both recognized the dark clouds on the horizon. Anna's father had warned her, soon before his death, that her time with Bukharin would be short but worth a whole lifetime.[43] His prediction was correct about duration but understated the trials and tribulations that lay ahead for his daughter.

CHAPTER 3

September 8, 1927:
Digging His Own Grave

W HEN THE STALIN-KAMENEV-ZINOVYEV troika fell apart in early 1926, the ever-agile Stalin formed a new majority with Bukharin, Rykov, and Tomskii. In response, his former allies, Kamenev and Zinovyev, joined forces with the aloof Trotsky to form the United Opposition. Stalin feared that the charismatic Trotsky, the fiery Zinovyev, and the lawyerly Kamenev would be formidable rivals if they combined forces. He needed to get them out of the way for good. In this endeavor, Stalin could count on Bukharin, who had clear ideological differences with the United Opposition's program of forced industrialization, hostility to peasant agriculture, and opposition to alliances with European social democrats, as well as its complaints of weak support for the Chinese communists.

Stalin's own policy positions fluctuated according to political expediency. In fact, he would soon adopt Trotsky's position as his own. At this point, however, he needed a pretext to remove the United Oppositionists from power.

Major decisions were still being made by majority vote of the Politburo, with Central Committee plenums called to ratify major Politburo decisions; the plenums could nonetheless be contentious and required careful preparation. There were nine full (voting) members of the Politburo. Of these, Stalin could rely on the faithful V. M. Molotov and could intimidate three other "neutral" members. The alliance with Bukharin gave him a comfortable majority.

Stalin controlled the party machine, and Bukharin and his group delivered the necessary Politburo votes.

Stalin knew that alliances could shift. If he had political enemies, it was best to eliminate them permanently. He had not yet the power to kill them, but removal from the party was the next best thing. As of 1926, no Politburo member had been expelled. The only way to leave was to die, sometimes quietly expedited by Stalin. Removing the civil war hero, Trotsky; the head of the Leningrad party and Comintern, Zinovyev; and Lenin's former right-hand administrator, Kamenev, was a daunting task, but one Stalin was prepared to take on. What he needed was to catch the United Opposition in a "crime" against the party that would justify Draconian punishment.

The crime he settled on was "factionalism." In Stalin's vocabulary, that meant advocacy of any policy that differed from his own. Conveniently for him, Bukharin, not Stalin himself, could lead the attack. After a fiery Bukharin speech against Trotsky at a party forum in 1926, Stalin called out: "Well done, Bukharin. He does not speak; he slashes."[44]

The factionalism charge was not new. Stalin had maintained that all loyal party members must accept the "unified party line of the Central Committee," an organization that he conveniently headed. Trotsky, Kamenev, and Zinovyev were free to voice their opposition within the Politburo; but if they publicly opposed the official line, they were "splitting the party." If the United Opposition accepted Stalin's interpretation, of course, it held losing cards in this deadly game. Stalin had the party machinery under tight control, and with the help of Bukharin, he commanded a decisive Politburo majority.

The United Opposition's only chance was to appeal directly to the party. Party congresses, where the rank and file assembled with the elite, represented the ideal opportunity, and a congress was scheduled for the end of 1927. In stormy Politburo meetings of March, June, and October 1926, members of the United Opposition argued that they, as party members, had the right to present their platform directly to the congress and let the delegates decide the unified party line. Each time the challengers were defeated; they had to agree to support the line and admit that to do otherwise was a "deviation from Leninist principles."

Yet Trotsky, Zinovyev, and Kamenev continued to advocate an alternative platform, bringing matters to a stormy head in a fateful Politburo meeting on September 11, 1927.[45] For much of the debate, Stalin remained silent and let Bukharin do the talking:

> BUKHARIN: I wanted to make several remarks about the speech of Comrade Zinovyev. He uttered many terrible words. He said that the party is high-handed against the opposition. But I consider that it is the *party* that is being subjected to systematic attacks and aggression by the opposition.
>
> ZINOVYEV: You are not the party.
>
> BUKHARIN: I know I am not the party. Let's take, for example, your charge of "deceiving" the party. Would not any member of the party understand this hypocrisy? Look: you have admitted that your factional work is a procedural deviation from Leninism. Did you write this? Yes . . . and you gave your solemn promise to return to the correct path of Leninism. It was you who deceived the party.
>
> (An inaudible exclamation from Zinovyev.)
>
> BUKHARIN: Thieves always shout, "Catch the thief!" Zinovyev is always doing this. Before the Fourteenth Party Congress, he said: We are for the Central Committee, while all the while he worked against the Central Committee. Lenin more than once detected such tactics in his polemics with Trotsky, when he spoke of the "policy of schism covered with phrases of unity." You are now conducting the same policy, despite the fact that you admitted in your corrupt language that this is a deviation from Leninism. (Noise in the hall. Chairman rings a bell. An inaudible exclamation from Zinovyev.)

Bukharin then derided Zinovyev's claim that a small group of unauthorized "heroes" can represents the will of the party.

> BUKHARIN: Zinovyev makes a clever argumentation: the party is one thing; Stalin, X, and Y [the Bukharin group] are another. But there is something strange going on. Stalin and X and Y can carry decisions through the party. This is a misfortune, according to Zinovyev. But permit me: if you still have a shred of reason, you must ask yourself why certain people are able to dictate the will of the party . . .
>
> TROTSKY (interrupting): Our platform answers this question.
>
> BUKHARIN (ignoring the interruption): . . . and others, such as yourselves, are not able, although you have occupied the highest positions in the party! The answer is obvious, but it is not the answer in your

verbose and absurd platform. The answer is that the party considers proposals that are offered by one or another group of leaders, and the party decides. The party, Comrade Zinovyev, has by no means become a herd of sheep.

Stalin then could not resist baiting the infuriated Trotsky, whom he had detested since the civil war, when Trotsky accused him of bungling and disobedience on the battlefield:

STALIN: Comrade Trotsky demands equality between the Central Committee, which carries out the decisions of the party, and the opposition, which undermines these decisions. A strange business! In the name of what organization do you have the audacity to speak so insolently to the party?

ZINOVYEV: Each member of the party has the right to speak before the party congress—not only organizations.

STALIN: It is not permitted to speak so insolently as a turncoat to the party.

ZINOVYEV: Don't try to split us; don't threaten, please.

STALIN: You are splitting yourselves off. This is your misfortune. . . . Judge now the value of your idle chatter. . . . Only those who have joined our enemies could sink so low. But we wish to pull you out of this morass.

TROTSKY: You should pull your own self out of the swamp first. (Noise, shouting, the chairman's bell.)

That Politburo meeting ended with a draft resolution calling—implausibly—for party unity. The defeated Kamenev reluctantly formulated the key point: "Recognizing the factional battle within the leadership of the party as harmful—notice that I did not refuse to use the word 'harmful'—we call upon our supporters to refrain from and immediately cease any kind of factional struggle."

After extensive discussion of wording, those present voted on each of the points, with the stubborn Trotsky either abstaining or casting the sole negative vote. He declared, "I am not able to vote given such a formulation, which does not allow me to express my position either by voting yes or no or by abstention."

The September 1927 defeat of the United Opposition established the precedent that any alternative view now constituted factionalism (as defined by Stalin) and "betrayal of the party," prompting from the losers a bitter charge of cowardice:

ZINOVYEV: What are you afraid of? Why are you trying to hide our platform? What does this say about your courage?

STALIN: We are not prepared to turn the party into a discussion club.

That highly fractious Politburo meeting ended with the opposition "agreeing to establish peace within the party on the basis of the adopted resolution." The meeting's version of peace was short lived. When the United Opposition organized demonstrations two months later, they were expelled from the party, and mass expulsions of their allies followed. Trotsky was exiled to Alma-Ata in January 1928, followed by expulsion from the Soviet Union thirteen months later.

Stalin had rid himself of Trotsky, Lenin's "most capable" founder of Bolshevism. Trotsky would go on to pester Stalin from abroad until an assassin's axe caught up with him in Mexico in August 1940. Kamenev and Zinovyev were exiled to the remote provincial town of Kaluga. Their fates would continue to be intertwined with that of the Bukharins.

In that Politburo proceeding, Nikolai Bukharin had unwittingly helped dig his own grave. The September 1927 decision established that small groups opposed to the Central Committee (which Stalin controlled) were violating Leninist principles—a crime for which they could be expelled from the party. The "party" had in effect become Stalin, who controlled its machinery. Bukharin and his allies did not realize that they would soon find themselves standing in the shoes of those they had expelled.

CHAPTER 4

1926:
Stalin Plays an Unlikely Cupid

IKOLAI BUKHARIN'S three-room apartment in the Metropole was a meeting place for his students, colleagues, and political allies. The Metropole was a swanky hotel earlier frequented by the elite of czarist Russia. Lenin converted it into apartments and rooms for Bolshevik officials. Bukharin's widowed father, a retired math teacher, lived with him. The animal-loving Bukharin had turned an abandoned fountain in front of his apartment into a menagerie that housed at different times an eagle, a bear cub, and a marmoset. (Anna developed her own appreciation of animals from Bukharin, and in her case it eventually extended even to the rats in her cell.)

Anna lived with her family in the flat above the Bukharins. Anna's father encouraged her to go and see "Nikolai Ivanovich." During one such visit, she overheard Stalin, whose disappointment with his own son was palpable, ask Bukharin's father: "How did you make your son? I want to adopt your method. Oh, what a son, what a son!"[46]

After returning from a trip with her family and Bukharin to Sochi, the eleven-year-old Anna composed a poem to him ending with: "Without you I am always blue." Anna's amused father encouraged her to give it to Bukharin: "Excellent! Since you have written it, go take it to your Nikolai." The bashful Anna refused, so her father suggested they put the poem in an envelope and write on it: "From Iurii Larin."

Anna decided to ring Nikolai's doorbell, hand him the envelope, and run away. As she descended the stairs, however, she ran into Stalin on his way to see Bukharin. She thrust the envelope into his hands to give to Bukharin. Thus, through Stalin, she conveyed what she would later call her "childish confession of love." When she returned to her apartment, Bukharin was on the phone asking her to come down. She was too embarrassed to go.

In 1927, General Secretary Stalin insisted that Bukharin move to the Kremlin—prompting the devastated young girl to tell her diary that '27 was "the saddest year." She remained with her family in her cramped room. Thereafter, she had to have a pass to be admitted to the inner sanctum of the Kremlin through its massive gates. Anna began taking a longer route to school past the Comintern building, on Mokovaya Street, where she was likely to encounter Bukharin. Luck was with her more than once, and she would rush with joy to meet him.

The Stalin-Bukharin 1925–26 meetings that Anna witnessed as a precocious child served to create the Stalin-Bukharin bloc and lay the groundwork for strategy against Trotsky and his allies.

CHAPTER 5

Summer with Stalin (1927)

JOSEPH STALIN INVITED BUKHARIN; his wife, Esfir' Gurvich; and their daughter, Svetlana to spend the summer of 1927 in his summer house in Zubalovo. His motive? Perhaps he was simply following the old maxim: keep both friends and enemies close

Esfir' Gurvich was a strong-willed woman. Born in Latvia into a Jewish family, she studied architecture in Petersburg, became involved in revolutionary causes, and was sent to Ekaterinoslav in 1919 with two revolvers to evacuate the party archives before the advancing White Russian army. In Moscow, the twenty-four-year-old Esfir' lived with other young Bolsheviks on the fifth floor of the Metropole. She became engaged to Bukharin at Lenin's summer residence after Lenin asked the blushing Bukharin, "Well, Nikolai, will it soon be time to tie the marital knot?" Their daughter, Svetlana, was born in 1924.

The wary Esfir' did not want to spend the entire summer in Stalin's Zubalovo dacha. The note she received from Nadezhda Allilueva, Stalin's wife, more than confirmed the invitation: "Come. Josif does not like when he is not obeyed." Esfir' continued to resist until Stalin arrived in person to carry the Bukharins off, as if they were prisoners. Each workday morning, Bukharin and Stalin were driven from Zubalovo to the Kremlin in Stalin's gleaming Packard, leaving the Zubalovo wives and children to amuse themselves by means of a variety of quiet pastimes.

"Dacha," or summer cottage, was scarcely an appropriate description of the stately, two-story mansion. It contained twelve rooms and occupied five hundred square meters of living space. The spacious ground floor contained the common areas, including a billiard room. Nearby dachas were occupied by relatives of Stalin's wife, the Alliluevas, and by party officials. The Zubalovo wives and children spent their summer days together in conversation, games, walks, and gardening. A nearby special farm supplied the residents with fresh vegetables and dairy products

By the end of the summer, due to disagreement over agricultural policy, Bukharin's relationship with Stalin began to deteriorate. Life in Zubalovo also did not contribute to good relations. Esfir"s concerns about living with the Stalins under one roof proved on the mark. As housemates, Nikolai and Esfir' witnessed Stalin's growing psychological and physical abuse of his wife. Esfir' and Nadezhda became close friends and intimates, and both Bukharins soon knew too much for Stalin's comfort. Bukharin himself would later report that Nadezhda often ran to him for protection from her abusive husband.

The two young Svetlanas (Stalin's and Bukharin's daughters bore the same first name) were unaware of the growing tension. Stalin's Svetlana remembered the wonderful children's playground, with its swings, slides, and tree house accessible by ladder. Her brother, Vasilii, usually had a guest to play with, while Svetlana had her own Svetlana—or Kozia, as she called her.

Svetlana Allilueva (Stalin) remembered a playful Bukharin whom the children all adored. Not only did he play with them, but he also filled the dacha with animals—hedgehogs on the balcony, foxes in the park, a hawk in a cage. ("Bukharin's foxes" outlived him and would populate Zubalovo grounds for years afterward.) Svetlana Gurvich remembered one incident that summer when the mischievous Vasilii Stalin bit the hand of Bukharin's brother, Vladimir, for no reason. Without thinking, Vladimir grabbed him and gave him a spanking. Stalin saw this from the house but said nothing. (Vasilii's childhood behavior was an omen: he died of alcohol poisoning in internal exile after serving years in jail for graft.)[47]

The summer of 1927 was a period of transition in Nikolai Bukharin's relationship with Stalin. It began with a sense of kinship with respect to policy and also a cautious feeling of friendship for Stalin. By the end of the summer, Bukharin understood that Stalin was odious and sadistic in his treatment of his wife. He also began to understand that Stalin did not share his political views. He probably now understood that Stalin used their alliance for his convenience. It would not have required much imagination to understand that Stalin would recruit new allies and turn them against him.

CHAPTER 6

June 1928:
"You and I Are the Himalayas"

WHEN TROTSKY, ZINOVYEV, AND KAMENEV were sent into exile in January 1928, Stalin was left to manage an increasingly uneasy alliance with Bukharin, Rykov, and Tomskii. A unified party line had to be forged, even though Politburo members now saw the world through different eyes.

Bukharin and his allies supported the status quo of peasant agriculture and a mixed economy; that is what they had fought with Trotsky about. Kremlin policy, as Bukharin said at an April 1925 conference, should encourage peasant families to "enrich themselves."[48] He also opposed industrialization at the expense of agriculture and favored balanced economic growth ("Tell me how to produce steel without grain").[49]

The first open break came in a letter to the Politburo from an old Bolshevik, Moisei Frumkin, protesting Stalin's agrarian policies of applying force and discriminatory taxes on the peasantry. The letter claimed that hundreds or even thousands of party members felt the same way. According to party rules, the Politburo was obligated to deliver a collective answer within a week. The irate Stalin, however, responded directly in his own name.[50]

Stalin knew that Bukharin had similar complaints but did not want to acknowledge them. In meetings, Stalin avoided open discussion of these issues, and he rejected Bukharin's pleas to meet face to face to sort things out. For the record, the frustrated Bukharin began sending letters that the general secretary could not ignore.

After receiving Bukharin's second missive, Stalin called "Bukhar-chik" to his wood-paneled Kremlin office.[51] He planned to keep Bukharin quiet by flattering him.

According to Bukharin's account, Stalin told him that the two of them towered above the rest of the Politburo: "You and I are the Himalayas—the others are nonentities." The two intellectual giants of Bolshevism, he declared soothingly, should bury their differences and dictate to those "others." What else was said has been lost to history, but it became clear that "Himalaya" Bukharin was not to be won over so easily by "Himalaya" Stalin.

Stalin's praise was supposed to remain between the two of them. But when at the next Politburo meeting, Stalin, in Bukharin's words, proceeded to "orate against me," the agitated Bukharin could no longer restrain himself. He blurted out that Stalin had only recently equated the two of them to the Himalayas while calling the others "nonentities." The startled Stalin lost his composure and screamed at Bukharin: "You lie! You invented this story to poison the other members of the Politburo against me."[52] Bukharin's revelation changed no minds. Virtually all members of the Politburo were becoming increasingly afraid to cross the Master (as both friends and foes commonly referred to Stalin).

One of the few people with whom Bukharin could speak freely about political problems was Anna's father, Iurii Larin, and after telling Larin the Himalayas story, he asked the older man: "Who do you think they believed? Me or Stalin? Larin's response: "Stalin, of course. No one wants to be a nonentity."

"Himalaya," in fact, became a running joke in conversations between the two of them. Thereafter, Bukharin and Larin used the term "Himalaya" with the special meaning of "avoiding mistakes," such as "Don't make any more Himalayas."[53] Larin's wife, Lena, was also in on the joke. She made the mistake of relating it to an acquaintance, who passed it along to the secret police. Within a short time, Stalin called in Bukharin to rebuke him for spreading slanderous rumors. Lena Larina, Stalin said, "is an honest woman and would not lie." Thereafter, Iurii would facetiously call his wife "the honest woman."[54]

Iurii Larin died of a lung inflammation in January 1932—before Stalin could exact his revenge. Had he lived, he would have been one of Stalin's victims. Someone that close to Bukharin would not have been allowed to live.

It seems odd that the cunning Stalin miscalculated that he could win over Bukharin by flattery. He may have believed Lenin's comment that Bukharin's positions were etched in soft wax. In any case, this time flattery failed, and in the future, Stalin would resort to force. More broadly, it was growing increasingly clear that Stalin's and Bukharin's paths had diverged and that their differences could not be painted over by superficial measures.

CHAPTER 7

July 4–12, 1928: Bukharin Fights Back

Trotsky, Kamenev, and Zinovyev were no longer around to challenge Stalin. Only the Right Opposition, headed by Bukharin, still stood in the way of his drive to one-man rule and enactment of his radical policies.

Removing Bukharin and his allies from the Politburo was not easy. Unlike Trotsky, who was widely disliked, Bukharin, Rykov, and Tomskii were on good terms with other party leaders. (Bukharin's status was also bolstered by his position—which Stalin envied—of party theorist.) Attacking this trio of leaders without grounds would carry risks. If Stalin pushed too hard, they could go public—Bukharin through *Pravda* or through the Comintern, and Tomskii through the trade unions—and throw the party into dangerous turmoil. To win this battle, Stalin had to play his cards just right and hope for a major tactical error from his opponents.

For their part, Bukharin, Rykov, and Tomskii now had to fight back. Stalin's Politburo cronies had quietly begun the destruction of peasant agriculture. Worse, a majority in the Politburo was building against Bukharin and his allies. Stalin had replaced the expelled United Oppositionists with hard-core supporters.

Stalin launched his attack at the July 4–12, 1928, plenum of the Central Committee.[55] The nine-day plenum meant that the party was discussing an issue of fundamental importance. And although discussions within the Politburo were top secret, with transcripts produced on few agenda items and circulated narrowly, Central Committee plenums drew some two hundred delegates and invited officials. Open splits within the top leadership could scarcely be concealed, and although Stalin had stacked the Central Committee, the Bukharin group still had a solid share of supporters in the audience.

Stalin could not embark on his plans for forced collectivization and all-out industrialization without at least the semblance of a united party. Such radical and costly moves could not be seen as his decision alone. Somehow he had to get the plenum to accept his policies without driving Bukharin and his allies into open opposition—a challenging balancing act.

Rumors were already circulating about a schism within the Politburo. Stalin's nightmare was that Bukharin, as head of the Comintern, would announce his opposition before foreign communists. Bukharin, using this lever, wrote to Stalin before the plenum: "I told you that I don't want a fight. Let's carry out the plenum without unnecessary rifts and without generating whispered gossip."[56] In public, Stalin blamed rumors of schisms on "the hidden opposition which always is able to infiltrate meetings of party activists."[57]

Bukharin reported to Stalin, probably with some satisfaction, that "rumors of my candidacy for deportation to Alma-Ata"—then Trotsky's place of exile—were circulating among foreign communists.[58] Yet he agreed with Stalin that their differences should be kept quiet. The general secretary rewarded that friendly gesture by moving to deprive Bukharin of his international podium. In typical Stalin fashion, the process required patience and careful planning. It was not until April 23, 1929, that the "plenum of the Central Committee decreed . . . to remove Comrade Bukharin from his position in the Comintern."[59]

As 1928 began, Bukharin, Rykov, and Tomskii were at the peak of their power. They had expelled their ideological opponents with Stalin's help. Stalin had not yet revealed the full extent of his agenda, which they would have opposed with vigor. As head of the government, Rykov chaired Politburo meetings as well as Central Committee plenums. Tomskii headed the trade unions, which, in theory, had the right to vote on issues before the Central Committee. Bukharin headed the Comintern, and he set the tone of party ideology as editor of *Pravda*. Yet the three were increasingly aware that they faced a tough fight. As loyal party members, they felt obliged to observe party discipline, although Stalin did not. They began to question, however, whether keeping high-level disagreements within the Politburo amounted to loyalty or simply cowardice.

The balance of power on the nine-man Politburo was perilous for Bukharin's group. Stalin now had three solid votes plus his own. Bukharin and his allies had three total; to win, they had to get all of the body's possibly neutral members to side with them.

The prospects of that happening looked dim. Central Committee plenums were complicated affairs. In addition to Politburo members, a large number of regional party leaders were on the agenda. Speakers were interrupted by hecklers or supporters. Resolutions were drafted by compromise commissions, which presented their drafts for perfunctory approval. Votes to expel a member were in writing, often accompanied by a justifying statement. It was Stalin's machine that counted votes. It would thus be an act of bravery to vote against Stalin in such a setting.

Stalin had used the charge of factionalism to defeat Trotsky. He needed a similar charge against Bukharin and his allies, but any unprovoked move would give credibility to Tomskii's claim that Stalin was the true "Raskol'nikov" (splitter) of the party.[60] Stalin needed to goad his opponents into a trap. He did, and it was the volatile Bukharin who fell into it.

The plenum battle focused on the extraordinary measures being used by Stalin to "collect" grain in the countryside. "Extraordinary measures" were code words for forceful confiscation of grain by the secret police (OGPU), the militia, and local party activists. Such measures were being justified as necessary to overcome "grain collection crises" resulting from the peasants' understandable unwillingness to sell grain to the state at low prices. This debate had already taken place in the Politburo in more heated form. Both sides knew what to expect in the more public plenum, where transcripts were made for broader party consumption.

The plenum debate, which began on July 4, was remarkable for the absence of direct confrontations between Bukharin and Stalin.

They scarcely acknowledged each other's presence. Their battle played out largely through proxies. Anastas Mikoian, the commissar responsible for grain collections, initiated the discussion with an exhausting report, which began the morning of July 6 and continued through the evening.[61] Mikoian, a candidate (non-voting) member of the Politburo, was clearly on Stalin's team, despite Stalin's repeated abuses of him.

Stalin came out swinging three evenings later with a broad attack on those who "try to promote capitalist elements in the village in the name of preserving the peasant-worker alliance" and who "demand we remove extraordinary measures." The party must oppose "such anti-proletarian sentiments with all its strength and with all its means."[62]

In editing their remarks, speakers could insert new material to be read later by a wider audience. Stalin would later inject Lenin in the form of a rhetorical question: "Should not Lenin's slogan about reliance on the poor peasant, alliance with the middle peasant, and battle with the kulak (the Russian expression for wealthier peasants) be the basis for our work in the countryside?"[63] Stalin, however, conceded that it was probably time to end extraordinary measures, while leaving the door open to extending them: "Extraordinary measures are necessary and called for under extraordinary conditions, when we don't have other alternatives. Those who say extraordinary measures are bad under any circumstances are wrong."[64]

Stalin then berated "panic mongerers," who (like Bukharin) claim that extraordinary measures have severed the alliance between peasants and workers. "Grain difficulties" indeed created a "problem of a political character—even among certain segments of the poor and middle peasants."[65] But "it would be completely wrong to say we now have a 'disalliance' with the peasantry," as some, meaning Bukharin, have asserted. "Disalliance—this is the beginning of a civil war. It is not necessary to frighten with terrible words." He later added to his spoken comments: "There is no need to succumb to panic."[66]

These remarks are classic Stalin. They are delivered in a reasonable manner. They tell the audience that yes, we did use extraordinary measures, but at a time of true emergency ("we had no reserves") and with the support of the full Politburo. According to Stalin, the emergency was caused not by his policies but by those in the countryside hostile to Soviet power. His remarks went down well with the audience, which interrupted with exclamations of "Correct!" and "True!"

Nikolai Bukharin's turn to speak came the next morning—July 10. He rose to contradict Stalin on every point: extraordinary measures had alienated the poor and middle peasant; the alliance between the worker and peasant was threatened. Stalin's favorite scapegoat—the kulak—was not to blame. The number of kulak households was small and had scarcely increased over the years.[67] Grain output had fallen precipitously in areas where extraordinary measures had been applied.

Bukharin concluded: "We must immediately remove extraordinary measures which were historically justified and correctly enacted. They have outlived their time. But we now face a wave of mass unrest. There have been some 150 different uprisings throughout the union and dozens of terrorist acts [which he went on to describe]. Middle peasants are deserting to the camp of the kulaks." Bukharin concluded by citing the growing unease of party loyalists to warn that "We were victorious in gaining Soviet power, but we can also lose it."[68]

At this point, Stalin ally Lazar Kaganovich, and former head of the party in Ukraine, where much of the peasant unrest occurred, protested that Bukharin was exaggerating.

BUKHARIN (to Kaganovich): I could cite still more such examples given at the Central Committee plenum of Ukraine.

KAGANOVICH: There were other speeches there. You should cite them as well.

VOICE (a Bukharin ally)[69]: And the former general secretary of Ukraine, Comrade Kaganovich, comes here and doesn't say anything about this?

KAGANOVICH: Give me two hours like Comrade Bukharin, and I will tell you all and cite speeches.

BUKHARIN: When Lenin encountered panic mongers, he said they must be shot to maintain a united front. But he never said that we should keep quiet about facts. . . . I don't know whom I am contradicting. I only know that I learned about this widespread peasant unrest yesterday. . . . To get information on this business, I had to sit two days at the OGPU.

Despite the dead seriousness of the moment, a note of levity was introduced by a top Ukrainian party official, playing on Bukharin's use of the term "sit" (slang for "sit in jail"). When he asked Bukharin: "And for what did you 'sit'?" Viacheslav Menzhinskii, the head of the OGPU, quipped: "He 'sat' for panic mongering."[70]

After the break, Stalin's alter ego, V. M. Molotov, took the podium. He, like Stalin, cleverly left the back door open for extraordinary measures: "We cannot force the peasant to sell at unfavorable prices; that was the discredited idea of the Trotskyites. However, giving too much means capitulation to the kulaks and speculators. If the peasants are not satisfied with our price concessions, they again will not sell. Maybe someone [like Bukharin], out of naiveté, will describe this as a way to strengthen the union between workers and peasants."[71]

To the more than one hundred fifty delegates to the July 1928 Central Committee plenum, the deep split within the Politburo was evident. Yet there could only be one party line. Someone had to cobble together a resolution that could be passed unanimously. All loyal party members had to work for this compromise, which required the impossible task of fitting Bukharin's call for a free grain market with Stalin's extraordinary measures.[72]

In typical Bolshevik fashion, a drafting team of Bukharin and Molotov was named to prepare a resolution for the plenum. Drafting sessions consisted of Bukharin sitting all day at a writing desk while Molotov played billiards and got instructions from Stalin in the evening.[73] In the end, the commission agreed on a common set of resolutions (which left out Bukharin's "disalliance" and "free grain market"), and the party issued a unity statement.[74] By voting for the resolution, Bukharin put himself on record that the Politburo was united. He would shortly have to answer for his vote.

CHAPTER 8

Autumn 1928:
Pity Not Me

THE JULY PLENUM ENDED with Bukharin and his allies reaffirming party unity in exchange for the lifting of extraordinary measures and higher grain prices, with the bitter knowledge that Stalin was likely to renege. Bukharin left the plenum on the morning of July 11 in a foul mood, about to give Stalin the excuse he had been waiting for.

The July 1928 plenum brought home to Nikolai Bukharin that he was fighting a battle he was likely to lose. Anna found him lying on a sofa in the anteroom to his study, looking haggard and depressed. "How good that you have come, Larochka," Bukharin said, "I am in a bad way. Cats are clawing at my soul and giving me no rest. Do you understand me?"

He answered the question himself: "No, you don't understand me; you are so young. How good that you cannot comprehend everything." Bukharin's face had lost its radiance and looked gray. Anna broke down crying and blurted out: "I am so sorry for you, but I cannot help you in any way." After a pause, Bukharin responded: "Don't feel sorry for me, Larochka. Feel sorry for the peasant."[75]

Bukharin's solicitude for the peasants proved prophetic. Stalin's launch of forced collectivization in late 1929 depleted agriculture of livestock, deported Russia's best farmers to Siberia and Kazakhstan, and set off a famine that claimed more than five million lives, largely in Ukraine.[76] Traveling through Ukraine during collectivization, Bukharin witnessed its destruction firsthand. He gave all his money to children with swollen stomachs begging at each train station. He returned to Moscow in a deep state of depression, asking Iurii Larin, "What was the point of the revolution?"[77]

CHAPTER 9

Autumn 1928:
A Fifteen-Year-Old "Co-conspirator"

Anna Larina was in her fifteenth year as 1928 drew to a close. Several months had passed since the July plenum that left the man on whom she doted so depressed. A rare photograph from this period shows her with a coy smile, prominent and luminous eyes, a woolen cap covering her hair and ears, dressed in a dark overcoat—the very picture of a child of the Bolshevik elite. Drawn to Nikolai Bukharin "as a plant to the sun,"[78] Anna was a frequent visitor to Bukharin's bustling apartment in the Kremlin.

Although she later could not recall even the rough date, it must have been autumn, because she remembered that people were wearing overcoats and hats. The bell rang, and in rushed Aleksei Rykov, the prime minister and Bukharin's closest political ally. Rykov's heavy black beard, moustache, and perpetual frown gave him the appearance of a stern schoolmaster. Usually outwardly calm, Rykov entered the room in a state of extreme agitation. Stalin had just informed him that Bukharin was negotiating with the expelled Lev Kamenev to form a coalition to remove Stalin, who accused Rykov and Tomskii of supporting these negotiations.[79] Rykov's agitation was understandable: a Politburo member negotiating with an ally of the disgraced Trotsky and disclosing top-secret Politburo matters was akin to treason.

As Rykov recounted his meeting with Stalin, Anna saw Bukharin turn pale and his hands and lips tremble as he blurted out: "That means that Kamenev informed. There is no other way this could have become known." Rykov's worst fears were thus confirmed. Bukharin had indeed had a secret and frank political meeting with an expelled party member. Rykov became so enraged that he burst out such stuttering, hurling epithets at Bukharin as "little boy, little Bukharin," a "silly woman, not a politician," and chastising him for "baring his soul" to such a man.[80]

The shocked Anna listened as Bukharin recounted his side of the story. He and Grigorii Sokol'nikov (a former Trotsky ally and childhood friend of Bukharin) met with Kamenev in his Kremlin apartment on July 11. (Bukharin first claimed they met by chance on the Kremlin grounds.) Kamenev was again in Moscow after his exile in Kaluga. He had recently been restored to party membership by a special vote of the Politburo and was seeking another party job— a prize that only Stalin could award.

Upset by Stalin's actions at the plenum, Bukharin burst into an emotional tirade. He told Kamenev that he had been right at the 1925 party congress when he advised delegates not to reelect Stalin, "an unprincipled intriguer, who purposely stirs up discord."[81] He went on to chronicle his own complaints against the general secretary. How much he said would remain a matter of dispute.

Now, arguing with Rykov, Bukharin justified the Kamenev meeting by saying he wanted to dispel a rumor Stalin was floating that Bukharin had voted against Kamenev's reinstatement. Bukharin feared that Stalin would use Kamenev's anger against Bukharin to his advantage.

Anna's eyewitness account confirms a number of facts that Stalin would later deny: Bukharin's meeting with Kamenev took place without the approval of his allies, who were outraged when they learned of Bukharin's blunder; Stalin knew about the meeting shortly after the fact, although he would later pretend that he learned about it along with everyone else from an underground Trotskyite circular. Kamenev was the likely informer, as Bukharin suspected; Kamenev could have offered Stalin dirt on Bukharin in exchange for his reinstatement. If so, this mistake might have cost Kamenev (who had told Bukharin he only wanted a "quiet life")[82] his own life.

Kamenev, for his part, immediately understood the importance of the meeting. That evening, he recounted it in a letter to Zinovyev in Kaluga. Kamenev was to later make the unlikely claim that his letter had been intercepted by a Trotskyite organization. The more likely culprit was the OGPU or Kamenev. In any case, Stalin would wait five months to demolish Bukharin and his allies with this information.

Young Anna Larina was eyewitness to the genesis of the "Anti-Soviet bloc of Rightists and Trotskyites," which Stalin claimed was formed in the "negotiation" between Nikolai Bukharin and Lev Kamenev during their meeting. Her future husband, along with twenty other members of the "bloc," would be tried and in most cases executed in the final Moscow Show Trial of March 2–13, 1938. By this time, she herself would be buried deep within the Gulag.

CHAPTER 10

January 23, 1929:
"To a New Catastrophe with Closed Eyes"

O N JANUARY 23, 1929, almost a half year after Bukharin's meeting with Kamenev and three months after Rykov burst into his apartment, a shadowy Trotskyite organization distributed a leaflet entitled, "The Party Is Leading to a New Catastrophe with Closed Eyes."[83] To Bukharin's dismay, the leaflet quoted freely from Kamenev's supposedly purloined notes of their emotional conversation of the previous July 11, which were attached to the leaflet.

Written not as complete sentences but as cryptic phrases and key words, the notes shattered the myth of Politburo unity, with entries like: "Bukharin's break with Stalin is final. . . . Stalin's only interest is power. . . . Stalin does not let the Politburo discuss significant issues, Bukharin and Stalin are no longer speaking. . . . The blood of uprising will be spilled. . . . What can we do when we have an enemy like Genghis Khan?"

Even more incriminating is that Bukharin appears to have been speaking not only for himself: "I, Rykov, and Tomskii in one voice formulate the situation as such: it would be much better if you and Zinovyev were on the Politburo in place of Stalin."[84] Other Politburo members are described as double dealers, switching loyalty right and left. Sergo Ordzhonikidze, industry czar and Stalin ally, is purported to curse Stalin to Bukharin's face but then to support Stalin in public. Politburo member Mikhail Kalinin betrays Bukharin at the last minute. Others are described in unflattering terms—for example, Molotov as a "lead butt."

Kamenev's notes show that he reserved the key question for the end of their conversation: "What do you want from us?" Bukharin's answer would determine whether he was simply venting or was "negotiating the creation of a political bloc," as Stalin would claim. Kamenev's notes could be interpreted either way. They contain such phrases as, "The question of Stalin's removal has been raised" and "Bukharin wishes to speak with Zinovyev about a bloc to remove Stalin." Bukharin's direct response to Kamenev's question, however, was: "Stalin is boasting that he has you and Zinovyev in his pocket. You can decide your own course, but I request that you do not help him destroy us. Stalin will likely seek contact with you, and I wanted you to know what is at stake."

According to Kamenev, Bukharin warned that the OGPU was watching; Kamenev should not seek to contact him again. Unfortunately for his allies, Kamenev's notes have Bukharin again adding: "Only Rykov and Tomskii know about this."

Bukharin's meeting with Kamenev, as a potentially serious violation of party rules, ended up on the desk of Ordzhonikidze (whom the notes claim was a double dealer). Comrade Sergo, the head of the party's Central Control Commission, promptly demanded written accounts from those who took part in the meeting. Kamenev submitted his letter on January 27; Sokol'nikov, Bukharin's childhood friend who arranged the meeting, sent his the next day. Bukharin refused to send his account. Instead, he stubbornly prepared a "declaration"—which Stalin would henceforth refer to as the "Bukharin Platform"—three days later.[85]

Neither Kamenev's or Sokol'nikov's letters denied that at a minimum, Bukharin had disclosed Politburo secrets. At a maximum, he had met with an opposition figure to plan the overthrow of the general secretary of the party. Thereafter, Stalin would refer to the meeting as a "negotiation," while Bukharin would call it a "conversation."

Stalin's call for an emergency joint session of the Politburo with the Central Control Commission set off a firestorm in the Bukharin camp; Rykov and Tomskii walked out of two Politburo meetings convened to condemn Bukharin's alleged treachery, and the accused protested the attempt to ruin his "party name." Stalin's calm justification: "If workers in factories are hearing about conflicts within the Politburo, we must let the Central Control Commission know. . . . This meeting is not a kangaroo court. The question of Comrade Bukharin's political fate will not be decided here."

In his July 30 declaration, Bukharin questioned the accuracy of Kamenev's letter, citing wrong dates, incorrect facts, and other suspicious elements, but he did not deny the "open and frank" conversation: "I made a mistake to open up to Kamenev. I didn't anticipate that this conversation could be used in such an underhanded way." His letter ends by proffering his resignation: "I consider that it is necessary to free me from my work in the Comintern and *Pravda*. So that the party is not harmed, I'll accept any suitable form of retirement."[86] Notably, his resignation did not include his Politburo membership.

Bukharin also "categorically denied as nonsense and defamation" that he opposed the party line.[87] He claimed to support in full the party's "literal resolutions" (many of which he authored), but said that actual policy had contradicted them "on the basis of instructions or speeches of certain comrades [Stalin] who understand the situation in their own way."[88] Thus, Bukharin could indeed support the party line while complaining to Kamenev about disunity. But his was a tortured argument, and it fell on deaf ears.

Bukharin should have rested his case at that point, but instead he dug in his heels and counterattacked—aiming directly at the general secretary. Stalin's calls for "tribute" from the peasants to pay for industrialization was, Bukharin said, "military-feudal exploitation of the peasantry." He dug his grave deeper with this line: "No one has the right to demand that a member of the party accept the notion of tribute." Bukharin's final salvo was against Stalin's "bureaucratization" of the party (a Trotsky term he deliberately used to taunt Stalin). He declared that party secretaries are not elected but chosen by Stalin, trade union leaders are removed for voting against Stalin's appointees, and any concern about the crumbling alliance with the peasantry is branded as a deviation.

Bukharin's and Rykov's desperate maneuvers failed to prevent the convening, on January 30, 1929, of a special joint session of the Central Committee and Central Control Commission. This joint session knocked the remaining wind out of sails of the Right Opposition. Thereafter, few party leaders would dare to take the side of its members. Bukharin, Rykov, and Tomskii were disgraced.

CHAPTER 11

Early Warnings:
Stalin Is Dangerous

AS BUKHARIN PREPARED to attend the January 30, 1929, session that would render a judgment on his factional offenses, he certainly pondered what defeat would mean. At the time, it probably meant demotion to a lesser post. The worst prospect, exile, did not look so bad; the pardoned "factionalists" Kamenev and Zinovyev had already returned to Moscow from their exile in the remote city of Kaluga. Punishment by imprisonment or death for factionalism was not something even considered at the time.

Bukharin may have had additional reasons to think that Stalin would not harm him. At least on the surface, their personal relations remained cordial. Bukharin was one of a small circle of six or seven party officials who addressed Stalin informally,[89] and was often a guest at Stalin's dacha in Zubalovo even after his infamous meeting with Kamenev. Dressed casually in sandals and a peasant blouse, Bukharin played with Stalin's children, and his daughter, Svetlana, taught them to ride bikes and to shoot an air gun.[90]

As always, Stalin maintained an air of equanimity, calm, and reasonableness. But beneath this veneer boiled seething resentment, jealousy, rage, and a desire for revenge.

Early on, Bukharin understood the intensity of Stalin's jealousy: When a Politburo member objected to Lenin's 1919 decision to award Stalin the Order of the Red Banner alongside Trotsky, Bukharin explained to him: "Can't you understand? Stalin can't live unless he has what someone else has."[91] In the early 1920s, several party leaders began discussing what was the best thing in the world. One answered "books," another "women," a third "cognac." Bukharin answered: "Nothing compares with the feeling when you find yourself with thousands of others on the crest of a popular wave." Stalin's answer: "The sweetest thing is to devise a plan (against an adversary), then, being on the alert, waiting in ambush for a good long time, finding out where the person is hiding. Then catch the person and take revenge."[92]

Bukharin himself caught two rare glimpses of the unguarded Stalin, as later related by Anna.[93] The first occurred by chance after a Politburo meeting. Bukharin discovered that he had lost a pencil that he used for taking notes. He spied it in the empty meeting room next to a scrap of paper on the floor. It was a note in Stalin's hand that read, "Must destroy Bukharin's disciples." Evidently, Stalin had put his intention down on paper, accidentally dropped the note, and then forgotten about it.

The second revealing incident related to Stalin's wife, Nadezhda. Her 1932 suicide followed a banquet in which Stalin insulted her in public. Stalin was known to be abusive toward his wife, and he was wary of those close to her, including Bukharin's second wife, Esfir' Gurvich. In addition, he may have been jealous of Bukharin himself, whom Nadezhda considered one of her closest friends. Anna: "He [Bukharin] told me how once, by chance, he called at the dacha in Zubalovo when Stalin was not at home. Nadezhda was there, however, and they took a walk around the grounds. . . . Unbeknownst to them, Stalin arrived and crept up stealthily behind them. When they turned in surprise, he looked Nikolai Ivanovich straight in the face and uttered a terrible threat: 'I'll kill you.' Bukharin took this as a cruel joke, but Nadezhda shuddered and turned pale."

That Bukharin kept the scrap of paper from the floor of the Politburo meeting shows that he took the threat seriously. However, it would have been unclear at that time how Stalin would go about "killing" Bukharin. Capital punishment of party members was taboo (although it was being applied to non-party "wreckers" and "saboteurs"). As Trotsky, Zinovyev, and Kamenev faced Stalin's wrath, they surely felt that they were struggling for political, not physical, survival. Despite these earlier warnings, Bukharin probably concluded the same.

CHAPTER 12

Father and Daughter as Bolshevik Idealists

ANNA LARINA AND IURII LARIN were not related by blood; he was Anna's stepfather. Anna's mother was abandoned by her father, whom she never knew. She lost her mother to tuberculosis at the age of one and was sent to live with her mother's sister, Lena—the wife of Iurii Larin. But as Larin's stepdaughter, Anna inevitably became a true believer in the Bolshevik ideal of building a new socialist world.

Lena's father had not been enchanted with the marriage: "A beauty like that, and she married a cripple." As both Lena and Iurii disappeared into the revolutionary underground and then exile, Anna was brought up by her maternal grandfather in the small Belorussian town of Gory-Gorki. At the age of four, she began asking about her parents, and her grandmother answered with displeasure: "They prefer to sit in jail, to escape arrest by running abroad, to sitting here beside you and cooking kasha."[94]

When Lena came to visit Anna in early 1918, Anna was pleased that her new mother was so beautiful and elegant, nothing like the infidel revolutionaries her grandmother described. Lena left carrying pies baked by Anna's grandmother. She arrived at the Astoria Hotel in Petrograd, where Trotsky was meeting with Larin, just as the police arrived to arrest him; so the great revolutionary leader was carried off to jail bearing grandma's pies.

Anna was later to learn that Iurii Larin had been born under tragic circumstances. His mother contracted scarlet fever during her pregnancy, and he was born with cerebral palsy. His father abandoned his mother before his birth, and she went to live with her sister in Simferopol, the capital of the Crimea. By the age of nine, the crippling disease had advanced to paralysis on one side. Specialists in Berlin offered no hope; he was not expected to live to adulthood. Throughout his life, he had to walk with a cane, awkwardly throwing out his paralyzed leg in front of him and then thrusting his body forward. One arm and hand were fully paralyzed. However, he managed to write prolifically in an awkward scrawl.[95]

Living with her grandparents, Anna had not yet seen her father, but she received letters in which he wrote her fairy tales. They were signed "Your Papa." One was a parable about a colony of skinny mice exploited by fat mice—Anna's first lesson in Marxism. In March 1918, Anna's parents came for her. Anna, frightened by her stepfather's appearance, screamed, "I want to go to Grandpa!" She scurried under a sofa as Larin stood by patiently, flustered and red in the face. As Anna became accustomed to Larin's looks, she began to consider his face handsome, and she would help him dress. He could not put on a coat by himself. He became her beloved father.

As Anna grew up in the shadow of the Kremlin, her father's apartment and adjacent office served as meeting places for Larin's numerous state committees so that he did not have to make tortuous trips to other locations in Moscow. In their apartment, Anna observed firsthand the enormity of the task of creating the first Soviet state.

Anna became caught up in her father's enthusiasm and dedication for the Bolshevik cause. At a very early age, she developed a keen interest in the "internal life of the party"[96]—as well as an awareness that her favorite, Nikolai Bukharin, was also the party's "favorite." Anna read Bukharin's book, *The ABCs of Communism*, a gift from her father, at the age of thirteen.[97] A treatise on the abstract theory of socialism was certainly unusual reading matter for a teenage girl, but Anna had grown up among books. Iurii Larin was a bibliophile who had a massive library on economics and literature, which he purchased at used bookshops located beside the Kitai Gorod wall in the back of the Kremlin.

Anna's dedication to the socialist cause was heightened by stories of her father's revolutionary exploits. Despite handicaps that made him easily recognizable by the police, the young Larin directed student Social Democratic organizations in the Crimea until he was exiled to Yakutia in the far north. He escaped and took refuge in Geneva, where he joined the Mensheviks. Larin and Nikolai Bukharin became close friends in exile. They were neighbors in Switzerland from the summer of 1915 to the summer of 1916. After numerous arrests and imprisonments (including the notorious Peter and Paul Fortress in Petersburg and the infamous Metekh prison in Baku), Larin played a key role as a member of the Petrograd Soviet during the October Revolution.

After the Bolshevik victory, Lenin chose him to organize Russia's war economy. Larin's intellectual productivity exceeded that of many healthy men. His co-workers called him Maestro, as he did complex mathematical calculations in his head. (When Larin died, the Moscow Brain Institute took his brain for study.) Larin's vivid imagination caused an incredulous Lenin to write that "if the supply of Larin's fantasy were spread out evenly over the entire membership of the Russian Communist Party, that would be about right."[98] Larin combined his fantasizing with a quick sense of humor, as in his facetious piece in *Pravda* predicting that one day men could change into women and vice versa. In the article, his friend Nikolai Bukharin decides to become Nina Bukharina with a long flaxen pigtail but cannot turn back into Nikolai. This story had legs; in a later party biography, Nikolai Bukharin's wife was listed as "Nina Bukharina."

Larin also possessed a kind heart for the downtrodden. He was often petitioned by unemployed workers for jobs. A war widow raising three children asked him for money and, having none on him, he gave her Lena's arctic-fox coat.

Under her father's tutelage, Anna decided to study at a planning institute, where she could contribute to "socialist construction." Like her fellows, she joined the Communist Youth League, also called the Komsomol, and as she entered her teens, she regularly attended political lectures. As Anna grew into a young beauty, she attracted a number of admirers, including Zhenya Sokol'nikov, the son of Grigorii Sokol'nikov (whose fate would be intertwined with Bukharin's), who also lived in the Metropole. Later, Nikolai Bukharin would react with jealousy when he saw the two together.

Among young Anna's other admirers was Lavrentii Beriia, who would later become the head of the NKVD. At the age of sixteen, Anna traveled with her parents to Georgia, where she met Beriia, the head of the party. He had a reputation as a womanizer with a penchant for young girls, so it was no surprise when he said to Larin, "I never knew you had such a lovely little girl." Anna could only blush in shame. (The same Beriia, in December 1938, extended Anna's Gulag sentence after telling her she had "become extraordinarily beautiful" since he last saw her.)[99]

On his deathbed, Larin instructed Anna, "It's not enough to love Soviet power just because you live well as a result of its victory. You have to be ready to give up your life for it, or shed blood, if that is required. Swear that you can do it!" His final, mumbled words appeared to be "Scatter my ashes from an airplane" and "We shall be victorious."[100] As it happened, Larin died at a fortuitous time: his ashes were buried with full honors in the Kremlin Wall. Had he lived, he would have been shot along with his friend Bukharin and buried in an anonymous pit.

Had Anna's life followed a normal course, she would have become a member of the party and worked in a government job. Her marriage to Nikolai Bukharin in 1934 changed all that for the worse—much worse. She began living with a man whom Stalin was intent on eradicating.

CHAPTER 13

January 30, 1929 : "You Can Test the Nerves of an Elephant, Bukhashka"

A S THE ONE ONE-DAY SESSION of the Politburo and Central Control Commission on Bukharin's "negotiation with Kamenev" began on January 30, 1929, a number of attendees were on edge.[101] In Kamenev's notes, they had been accused of double dealing against Stalin. Among the nervous group: the gruff chairman of the meeting, Sergo Ordzhonikidze.

Bukharin hoped the chairman would be neutral in the proceedings. Those hopes were immediately dashed as Comrade Sergo brusquely reminded the audience that Bukharin had himself codrafted the "unity" resolution that had been adopted unanimously by the July plenum. He read aloud Bukharin's purported remarks to Kamenev and concluded: "These Comrades must tell us whether there is a unified party line. Personally I have doubt about this. . . . Bukharin asserts there was no talk of a bloc. If that is the case, we must ask why it was necessary to conceal the conversation from the Politburo."

Ordzhonikidze quickly denied Bukharin's claim that he had bad-mouthed Stalin. Other implicated party officials kept quiet but presumably trembled.

Only fragmentary records of this Politburo meeting survive.[102] Bukharin's exchanges with Stalin make clear that he felt he had been set up. Stalin was holding the newly rehabilitated Kamenev—his earlier sins forgotten—in the wings to testify. Now, according to Stalin: "Kamenev is a member of the party and will tell the truth."

In his usual reasonable and amiable manner, Stalin denied that there was any deal with Kamenev. Unlike Bukharin, he had refused to meet with Kamenev when the latter came asking for a job, turning the matter over to a "commission." All of this was done in the open, but "Comrade Bukharin hid his negotiations with Kamenev from the Politburo."

Stalin then turned to Bukharin's transgressions: "Comrade Bukharin assures us that he had no intention to create a political bloc with former oppositionists against the Politburo majority. But what basis do we have to believe him? If he had no such intention, why did he conspire against the Central Committee? Why did he hide his negotiations with Comrade Kamenev? When he said to Kamenev 'only Rykov and Tomskii know and you should tell no one,' is it not clear that Comrade Bukharin admitted the offense of negotiating with Kamenev?"[103]

Stalin feigned deep regret: "We thought that Bukharin and his supporters had rejected their mistakes and that disagreement was ended, but now it is clear that disagreement does exist."[104]

Stalin then issued his most damaging accusation: that Bukharin favored the capitalist class. Stalin asked, "Could it be that Comrade Bukharin is in favor of kulak elements?"[105]

Bukharin could contain himself no longer, addressing his adversary without the obligatory "Comrade": "Stalin, you are trying to tie a pro-kulak policy on me. I don't understand why that is necessary!"

Unfazed, Stalin built up to his conclusion: "Bukharin wants to resign his positions because the Central Committee does not carry out the resolutions which he himself accepted. But perhaps the problem is that the party line does not correspond to what he wants. But this means he is acting against the party line."[106]

The meeting ended with Stalin's proposal for a commission "to work out three directives: first, to censure Comrade Bukharin for his negotiations with Comrade Kamenev; second, to render a political evaluation of the mistakes of Comrade Bukharin; and third, to reject the resignations of Comrades Bukharin and Tomskii."[107] At this point, Stalin made a characteristic magnanimous gesture "to include Bukharin on the commission." Bukharin declined, then accepted, but the commission met without him.[108]

Its report, issued on February 9, condemned Bukharin's "discreditation of the party line." Bukharin, the report said, should cease and desist promoting a new party line favoring "capitalist elements." Both his and Tomskii's resignations were rejected, and the two were ordered to faithfully carry out all decisions of the party.[109]

Bukharin's crucial and inflammatory meeting with Kamenev had provided Stalin with the grain of truth needed to create the myth of a "Left-Right Opposition bloc." The meeting, the mysterious theft of Kamenev's letter, and the propitious appearance of the Trotskyite proclamation bear the markings of a Stalin setup. Indeed, Kamenev had spoken with Sokol'nikov about the meeting over a Kremlin telephone line that was monitored by the secret police.[110] So Stalin would have known all along what was going on. Bukharin's rage should have been directed at himself for falling into Stalin's trap.

CHAPTER 14

Summer of 1934: A Second Fateful Meeting

L EV KAMENEV WAS BORN LEV ROSENFELD in 1883, the son of a railway worker. He attended school in Tbilisi, where he met Stalin in radical revolutionary circles. His education at Moscow University was interrupted when he joined the revolutionary underground. Like other Bolsheviks, he took on a nom de guerre that suggested strength and hardness; the name "Kamenev" denoted "man of stone," while "Stalin" meant "man of steel." He was well connected with both Lenin and Trotsky: in exile, he was one of Lenin's top lieutenants; and he married Trotsky's sister, Olga, with whom he had two sons. All were to be executed on Stalin's orders.

On his return to Russia, Kamenev became a member of the Politburo and worked as Lenin's deputy. He ran the government during Lenin's protracted illnesses.

Bukharin's disastrous meeting with Kamenev on July 11, 1928, was not the only dramatic intersection in the two men's lives. In August 1936, Kamenev would testify that Bukharin had plotted with him to murder Stalin and other party officials.

Anna Larina, now Nikolai's wife, witnessed a second meeting between Bukharin and Kamenev in the summer of 1934, six years after their fateful "negotiation." She and Bukharin were driving to a rest home outside of Moscow, located on a former princely estate. As dinner was being served, Kamenev, unbeknown to them a guest at the rest home, joined their table. Kamenev was quite amiable, but Bukharin was reserved and, suddenly remembering urgent business in Moscow, stood up, said a hasty good-bye, summoned his wife, and drove off in haste. Bukharin then told Anna, "I beat it from Kamenev so as to not give him something to put in a transcript."[111]

Writing many years later, Anna characterized Bukharin's July 1928 conversation with Kamenev as a milestone in his life: "Bukharin at age forty-four finally got a full dose of what politics in the Stalin manner was all about. He became more circumspect ever afterward, and less trusting, even in his relations with Party comrades."[112]

CHAPTER 15

April 16–23, 1929: Waterloo

BUKHARIN KNEW THAT HE WAS FIGHTING a last-ditch battle. He could no longer hope to compromise with Stalin.

For his part, Stalin, with Bukharin and his allies muzzled, was now ready to move forward. But he also wanted to keep the myth of party unity alive a little longer. In a February 9, 1929, meeting in Stalin's office, Bukharin was offered "conditions" to persuade him to cooperate. Bukharin and his allies rejected them the same day, stating that Stalin should "heed the very wise advice of Lenin and not depart from collective leadership." The gloves were off, and the party knew it. Bukharin had accused Stalin of trying to create a one-man dictatorship.

Support remained for Bukharin in the party. As rumors spread of a rift, some activists showed their solidarity with him by echoing Bukharin's charge that Stalin was "torturing" the peasant along with the worker.[113] Stalin was still not ready to push through forced collectivization; he would wait another four months. The purpose of the April 16–23 Central Committee plenum was to destroy Bukharin.

The combined plenum of the Central Committee and the Central Control Commission of April 1929 was a hard-fought direct confrontation of the Bukharin and Stalin forces, but the outcome was never in doubt. Armed with Bukharin's "violations of party discipline," Stalin had the vast majority of delegates on his side. Shouts of "Correct!" or "True!" accompanied the speeches of Stalin and his supporters. The remarks of Bukharin, Rykov, and Tomskii were met with jeers and laughter.

This would be the last free-wheeling plenum of Stalin's lifetime. It opened with a lineup of his supporters heaping abuse on Bukharin for "hidden negotiations" and "prophesies of collapse" and demanding his removal from the Politburo with the prospect of "more decisive measures."[114]

The true fireworks began with Bukharin's speech on April 18. His address was a combination of brilliance and sharp attack undercut by tedious meanderings into abstract Marxist theory. Again, he said too much.

Bukharin had three goals: First, he wanted to lay out his political and economic plan as an alternative to Stalin's. Second, he wished to expose the flaws in Stalin's program. Third, and perhaps most important, he needed to rebut the charge of factionalism against him. Trotsky, Kamenev, and Zinovyev had been expelled on the same grounds; he could not allow this charge to stick if he wanted to remain in office. Bukharin had no illusions about the outcome, stating at the outset: "These will be my last remarks to you as a member of the Politburo."

Bukharin's main line of attack was against the use of force in the countryside. Extraordinary measures, he warned, were turning the peasants against the regime and were breaking the alliance between peasants and workers that Lenin had forged. Only market relations based on fair grain prices could lead to a prosperous and growing agriculture and preserve good relations between the Soviet regime and the countryside.

Bukharin reminded the delegates that Stalin himself, in "arias from another opera," had spoken in favor of a "permanent union with the middle peasant."[115] He then lashed out: "Comrade Stalin's attempt to convince us and me personally that we will unite the village against the kulak with extraordinary measures does not jibe with his earlier statements."[116]

Bukharin continued by warning that applying force in the countryside would reduce grain production."[117] He recounted an earlier conversation to make his point: "When I asked Mikoian about the winter sowing, he replied, 'Why do you spread panic? Peasants are sowing at night with lanterns with great enthusiasm.' In actual fact, they sowed less. Such are the abilities of Comrade Mikoian to foresee the future."[118] Unless peasants "can calculate and anticipate, they will do everything but grow grain."[119]

Next, Bukharin attacked Stalin's plan for "tribute" from the peasants to pay for industrialization. Bukharin knew that Stalin meant to gather tribute, either by confiscating grain or by forcing the peasants to sell at low prices dictated by the state. Hence, Stalin's "tribute" meant the exploitation of the peasant in a worker-peasant state, which Bukharin concluded was anti-Marxist and anti-Leninist.[120] Bukharin goaded Stalin into a rare exchange:

BUKHARIN: Why does Stalin insist on tribute—a clear mistake?
STALIN: And if Lenin used that expression?
BUKHARIN: There is nothing resembling Stalin's tribute in Lenin.
STALIN: That is not so.
BUKHARIN: No, it is so. The proletariat is not an exploiter of peasants and cannot be. To play with such terms is illiterate and harmful.[121]

Stalin fell silent, a sign that he felt himself on the losing end of this argument. He would get his revenge by humiliating Bukharin on the issue of tribute in the next plenum.

Bukharin then turned to his defense against charges, levied by Stalin in the December plenum, that both he and his ally Rykov were pro-kulak, that they wanted the kulak "to take root peacefully in socialism." The indignant Bukharin challenged the delegates to find any "taking root" reference in his speeches or writings. Rykov added: "I ask you to answer from which of my publications you are quoting. I assume that you are aware of the rules for the use of quotation marks and also the elementary rules of literary-political etiquette."[122]

Bukharin assured the delegates that the kulaks posed little or no threat anyway: "The number of kulak households is few, and we can allow individual farming to develop without fear of rich peasants."[123] He argued that if discriminatory policies were directed at the kulak, other peasants would be hit, again drawing Stalin into an exchange:

STALIN: But the kulak does not like extraordinary measures.

BUKHARIN: Of course, but unfortunately the middle peasant does not like them either. This Comrade Stalin has not noticed. But this is the heart of the matter.

As Bukharin began to rebut the charge of factionalism, the restive audience grew increasingly unruly. His remarks were interrupted by shouts, epithets, and jeering laughter. Bukharin had to plead to be heard; he put down a boisterous crony of Stalin's: "We all know your obedience to whomever is in the majority."[124] When the heckling seemed to be getting out of hand, he threatened to "walk out."[125] He launched a three-fold defense against the inflammatory charge that he had negotiated with Kamenev to form a bloc against Stalin:

First, he denied that he discussed with Kamenev removing Stalin and his supporters from the Politburo:

BUKHARIN: I deny emphatically that the question of forming a bloc was raised. Kamenev denies it, Sokol'nikov denies it.

STALIN: Kamenev does not deny the authenticity of his notes, and there he speaks about a bloc.

BUKHARIN: He denies two times in his letters that there was talk of a bloc, and, if I am not mistaken, there is no talk of a bloc in his notes or that I somehow "agreed" with Kamenev to change the composition of the Politburo.

ORDZHONIKIDZE: [In the notes] it is said that you would prefer Kamenev and Zinovyev to Stalin and Molotov.

BUKHARIN (irately): There "it is said." But I am absolutely not obliged to answer for everything that is "said" there.

ORDZHONIKIDZE: This is another matter.

Bukharin's second line of defense was that talk with Kamenev of forming a bloc against Stalin made absolutely no sense:

BUKHARIN: Explain this to me please how I could somehow "agree" with Kamenev to change the Politburo. What is this to mean? How is it possible for me and Kamenev to "change" the composition of the Politburo?

ORDZHONIKIDZE (in a rare moment of candor): It is true. That would be a major act of stupidity.

BUKHARIN: This would mean that Kamenev and I would have been playing some kind of a game in which we, bypassing the Central

Committee [which names the Politburo], somehow change the Politburo. I do not understand how this would be possible.[126]

Bukharin's third line of defense was to show that Stalin had lied
when he claimed that he had been shocked to learn from Kamenev's
notes that Bukharin disagreed with his policies. His most telling
moment came as he dramatically held up a letter he had written to
Stalin dated June 1–2, 1928—more than a month before his meeting with Kamenev:

> BUKHARIN: Some ask why I never talked about my disagreements?
> ORDZHONIKIDZE: Correct.
> BUKHARIN: Well, good. You are forcing me to read you a letter that I
> wrote to Comrade Stalin before the July 1928 plenum, in the first
> days of June.

Bukharin's letter opened with the following line: "I am writing
rather than speaking with you because it has become too difficult to
speak, and I fear you will not hear me to the end. But a letter you
will have to read." After that came a litany of criticism of Stalin's
policies: "We have no plan"; "We are unable to discuss substantive
matters even in small circles for fear of reprisal"; "Extraordinary
measures are turning into a new political line"; "We have destroyed
our central intellectual laboratory because we fear to discuss the
most important questions."[127]

Bukharin paused, then appealed directly to the assembly:

"Why do I read this letter? Because you had the audacity to say
to me: 'You are dishonest, without a conscience.'. . . But I say this
accusation is dishonest and without a conscience. Whether I spoke
or wrote or tried to knock on doors, I received no answer. . . . This
letter completely destroys the myth that no one wrote, that no one
knew of disagreements."

At this point, the heckling of Bukharin stopped. Delegates were
clearly puzzled.

> VOICE: Kamenev was after this letter?
> BUKHARIN: This was before any meeting. I said June 1.
> VOICE (supporting Bukharin): It matches.

Stalin, sensing a swaying of delegate opinion, quickly jumped in to control the damage of Bukharin's revelation.

> STALIN: Before the July plenum, there were arguments. We do not deny them.
> BUKHARIN: Maybe I should send old documents to the Central Committee to shed light on the merits of the accusations against me.[128]

Stalin, who controlled the agenda, waited four days (the evening of April 22) for the effects of Bukharin's defense to fade before he responded. Then he, as unquestioned Master, was greeted with sustained applause. The aggrieved Stalin brushed off the business of Bukharin's letter of June 1; he would refrain from "answering questions pertaining to my person."[129] Bukharin's letters, he declared, showed "that we are friends," but "friendship is friendship but duty is duty."

Such affronts were wearing poor Koba down in light of the enormous burdens that he had to bear: "Let the comrades from the opposition raise the question about freeing Comrade Stalin from his post. I think this would be the only question in which I would support them fully."[130]

In his usual organized fashion, Stalin then again ticked off Bukharin's transgressions,[131] concluding with feigned regret: "We have to look the matter straight in the eye, no matter how bitter. We have the revolutionary line of the party and the opportunistic line of the opposition."[132] Regrettably, Stalin continued, the party must purge itself to fulfill its tasks: "There are fishermen [such as Stalin] who, when the wind begins to blow, direct the boat against the waves in the right direction. There are others [such as Bukharin] who lie on the bottom of the boat and let it go where the wind takes it."[133]

Stalin then proceeded to dispute Bukharin's vision of agriculture. In contrast to Bukharin's village of poverty, Stalin's was a village of class struggle: "I say that dictatorship of the proletariat is necessary to defeat capitalism in the village, to carry out an uncompromising battle as kulaks attempt to take root."[134]

Bukharin, Stalin declared, does not understand the danger of the kulak: "An obliging bear is more dangerous than an enemy."[135]

Bukharin "denies that differentiation [the growing gap between rich and poor peasants] produces a capitalist class. We seek union with peasants, but not with any peasant—only with poor and middle peasants, and it is this union that will destroy class enemies and strengthen the working class."[136]

At this point, the assembly chairman proposed a break.[137]

> STALIN: "Really, have I spoken so long? I can continue. I don't need a break. Do you?"
> CHAIRMAN (hearing his master's voice): Let's vote. A majority? No break.

Gathering steam before a tiring audience, Stalin warned that to follow Bukharin, the state would have to keep raising prices until the peasant was satisfied, and the exploitive power of the kulaks would increase.[138] Moreover, "if the peasant does not sell enough, extraordinary measures must be applied. Yes, extraordinary measures do lead to some excesses, but we should not condemn the entire policy because of a few mistakes."[139]

Stalin denied Bukharin's charge that "tribute" is "exploitation" of the peasantry. "Tribute," Stalin soothingly explained, redistributes resources from agriculture into industry. "Maybe Bukharin does not recognize that we cannot manage without such a redistribution. Is this military-feudal exploitation? I am speaking about a kind of tax. Bukharin's reference to tribute reflects only his antipathy to our peasant policy."[140]

At this point, the supremely confident Stalin candidly explained how tribute was to be gathered by direct exchange (tractors for grain) between the collective farms and the state.[141] Stalin even conceded Bukharin's point that such an arrangement might reduce agricultural output: "Rightists do not care if agriculture develops on the basis of the collective farm or private household. It is all the same. For us, it is not all the same. Their main focus is to raise productivity. For us, most important is that the socialist sector outgrow the private sector."[142]

In Stalin's new alliance, the pesky individual peasant would be out of the way. Even extraordinary measures would no longer be necessary. Grain would be delivered by the collective farm, not by individual peasants. Stalin's explanation of how they would be "dragged into" collective farms had to wait until November.

Stalin was now ready to sum up. His first conclusion: "It is clear that we have a new opposition in the Bukharin group. This opposition intends to revise the line of the party, to prepare the soil to replace the party line with another line that is not and could not be considered the true line of the party."[143]

Second, Stalin brushed off Bukharin's charge that Stalin was abandoning the notion of collective rule in favor of one-man rule. "About the collective leadership: I know that our plenum can endure a lot, but there must be a feeling of shame when Bukharin says that we do not have a collective leadership."[144] In other words, the party was supposed to believe that major decisions were being made collectively, not by Stalin alone.

Third and most important, Stalin instructed the delegates on what should be done with the miscreants: They must "subordinate themselves to all decisions of the Central Committee. This is a minimum that ensures us a unity of will. . . . If we are to deal with this matter conscientiously, neither Bukharin nor Tomskii can remain in their posts in *Pravda*, the Comintern, and the trade union council. . . . This measure is unavoidable. It must be decreed: to free or more correctly remove Bukharin from his positions at the Comintern and *Pravda*."[145]

Stalin concluded on a note of feigned moderation, opposing those calling for their immediate removal from the Politburo: "I am against the removal of Comrades Bukharin and Tomskii from the Politburo. . . . I consider that it would be sufficient if we warned Comrades Bukharin and Tomskii that in the case of the slightest attempt to violate a decree of the Central Committee, these comrades will be immediately removed from the Politburo as violators of party discipline."[146]

These "mild" disciplinary measures, Stalin explained comfortingly, should be announced to the party but not published—in order "not to drag them by the scruff of the neck before the entire world but to give them the chance to correct themselves."[147]

Nikolai Uglanov, a Bukharin supporter and ousted Moscow party boss, fell for Stalin's "moderate" proposal:

UGLANOV (to Stalin): These are liberal measures.
STALIN (jokingly): We even make concessions to the middle peasant.
UGLANOV (continues the joke): Well, I am a middle peasant.
STALIN: Why not maintain a reserve of concessions for Uglanov.[148]

To stormy applause, Stalin closed the plenum on a magnanimous note: "We become here better comrades if we do not give in to feelings of indignation. If we leave Comrades Bukharin and Tomskii on the Politburo, we let the party know that we are not bloodthirsty, and we give them the opportunity to redeem themselves, if they are able to."[149]

In reality, Stalin was proposing slow strangulation, always dangling the prospect that things would turn out well if his opponents only mended their ways. Instead, within a few months, Bukharin, Tomskii, and then Rykov would "fail" their de facto probation and be removed one by one from the Politburo.

CHAPTER 16

1929–1931:
The Woman on the Train

S TALIN CONTROLLED FRIENDS and foe alike. As general secretary, he decided where each member of the party elite lived, when and where they would vacation or receive medical care, whether they could visit foreign countries, and—micro-management in the extreme—even the amount of money in their household budget. As general secretary, Stalin authorized travel of Politburo members and kept track of their movements. He secretly tapped their phones and monitored their meetings. When the July 1928 "conspiratorial" meeting between Kamenev and Bukharin was arranged over a phone line, Stalin's agents listened in.

Not surprisingly, then, little about Bukharin escaped Stalin's eye. In November 1928, after Bukharin had sought refuge from Stalin at a sanatorium in Kislovodsk, he was urgently called back to Moscow by his allies to resume the fight. As a Politburo member, Bukharin could and did order a special plane for the trip. But Stalin saw to it that the plane was twice ordered to land "for Bukharin's safety."[150]

The Master could also determine with whom Bukharin shared a bed. An intimate informer would pass on remarks or confidences to be used to blackmail or discredit. Bukharin's lover would have great credibility in relating any "anti-Soviet" remarks he made.

Bukharin's curious affair with Sasha Travina provides an example. It began shortly after his breakup with Esfir' Gurvich in the winter of 1929. Travina, it seems, happened to be in his sleeping compartment every time he took the night express train to Leningrad.

Knowing Stalin as he did, Bukharin must have been suspicious of this "coincidence," but he plunged into an affair with her anyway. The two proceeded to live together openly in an apartment separate from Bukharin's. They attended theaters and lectures as a couple. Some accounts even list her as his third wife.

A year and a half into their relationship, Travina confessed to Bukharin that she was a secret-police plant. She claimed she had fallen in love with him and had told her handlers she could not continue her spying. For his part, Bukharin would later claim unconvincingly, in a letter to Stalin from his cell, that he "knew she was close to secret-police circles, but this was not something that bothered [him]."

Instead, trouble came from another direction: "We were living together happily, but soon the same old thing started to happen. Nadezhda [first wife Nadezhda Lukina] began to spoil things, and Sasha and I began to suffer nervous paralysis. I was torn as a mad man between two sick people. I thought at one time it would be better to reject all form of private life. All these events tortured us, our souls were consumed, and we broke up."[151]

In his trial, Bukharin would be accused of organizing plots and coups during the very time he was together with Sasha Travina. His accusers were later to recount incriminating conversations on street corners or in private apartments that Travina could have overheard or at least known about. Bukharin apparently took some pains to make sure that she could *not* listen. One of his accusers testified: "My meeting with Bukharin took place in November of 1932 at Nikitinsky Square. We were walking along Tverskoi Boulevard towards Strastnaya Square. Bukharin made his excuses to Travina, saying that he needed to talk to me alone, and she left us."[152]

When Anna Larina later learned from one of Bukharin's associates that Travina was an informer, she took it as a sign that she and Bukharin could end up together.[153] And indeed, she must have known about Travina because the Bukharin-Larina relationship was so open. Larina understood perhaps even better than Bukharin that he could not stay together with an informant.

Clearly, the secret police would have placed a female informer in Bukharin's train compartment only on Stalin's orders. Yet Travina presumably revealed (or learned) little—because the trial records show no evidence from her used against Bukharin.

The name of Sasha Travina does not appear on Stalin's infamous execution lists; we do not know her ultimate fate. She went on to work as the deputy director of the department of scientific institutions (a job that Bukharin could have arranged with his connections).[154] Her name crops up again in the archives in a July 1937 letter recommending the firing of a science official, who was "not vigilant in the case of the former wife of Bukharin—Travina— who was expelled from the party."[155] Expulsion was usually followed by an NKVD investigation and then death or prison.

CHAPTER 17

August 1929:
Removal from the Politburo

I N THE SPRING OF 1929, Stalin pushed forced industrialization and collectivization through a compliant Politburo and Central Committee.[156] Despite the loss of his *Pravda* editorship, Bukharin refused to remain silent. He authored articles containing veiled criticisms of Stalin, using Lenin's own words to dispute the Master's policies. His tongue became looser: he complained of Stalin's rude behavior, such as interrupting a foreign communist and yelling at him to "go to hell,"[157] and he told others that Stalin's wife had appealed to him for help against his abuse.

Still smarting, Stalin used the July plenum to exact revenge for Bukharin's insulting accusation at the April plenum that he was "exploiting" the peasantry. From the podium, Stalin asked Bukharin whether he still considered tribute collected from the peasants to be "military-feudal exploitation." Bukharin replied that tribute in the form of low agricultural prices is "in my opinion military-feudal exploitation of the peasantry." Stalin, given the opening he sought, proceeded to pounce on Bukharin:

STALIN: Lenin more than once advised Bukharin to study Marxism, to seriously study political economy, but Comrade Bukharin did not want to follow the advice of our great leader. As a result of his political illiteracy and his confidence in his own genius, he has fallen into an extremely uncomfortable position. This happened today as well. If he seriously and systematically studied Marxism and political economy, he would likely have known that the system of low relative grain prices was not introduced by Stalin but by Lenin. He would have known that this was not military-feudal exploitation of the peasantry, but a tough, objective necessity. Russia is an agrarian country. Therefore the foundation of its capital is in agriculture.

BUKHARIN: This is a known truth.

STALIN: See, even Bukharin knows this. (Jeering laughter from the audience.)[158]

Because Stalin could ill afford any form of opposition, no matter how weak, to rally critics, he initiated in late August a coordinated attack against Bukharin, the leader of the "right deviationists." Bukharin was denied access to the press and could no longer respond to attacks.

The November 10–17, 1929, plenum of the Central Committee administered the final coup de grace to Bukharin. He (along with Tomskii and Rykov) had remained token members of the Politburo, but he was expelled from the Politburo on the last day of the plenum.[159] As a last-ditch attempt to save themselves, Bukharin, Tomskii, and Rykov signed a half-hearted admission of political error on November 25: "Recognizing our mistakes, we will conduct a decisive struggle against all deviations from the party's general line and above all against the right deviation."[160]

That did not satisfy Stalin. Having dispensed with Bukharin, he took his time removing Tomskii and Rykov from the Politburo. A Stalin appointee, Ivan Kabakov, the Urals party secretary, formally led a stealthy ouster of Tomskii at the Sixteenth Party Congress of July 1930:[161]

KALININ (presiding): The election of the Politburo is the first order of business. Are there any proposals?

KABAKOV: For Politburo members: Stalin, Kalinin, Rudzutak, Kuibyshev, Voroshilov, Rykov, Kaganovich, Kosior, Kirov [no mention of Tomskii].

KALININ: How do we propose to vote, separately or all at once?

VOICES: All at once.

KALININ: We'll vote en bloc. (Laughter).

VOROSHILOV: Explain what this means?

KALININ: It means together, as a whole. Those who are for the proposal raise their hands. Against? The proposal is carried. Accepted unanimously.

Seconds later, Kalinin asks Kabakov for his nomination for the post of general secretary:

KABAKOV: General Secretary, Comrade Stalin. (Voices: "Of course.")

Rykov, the last survivor, continued to serve as the prime minister, but after his speech of September 10, 1929, received sustained applause, Stalin decided that the "comedy of a non-party bureaucrat presiding over us cannot continue."[162] He replaced Rykov with the loyal Molotov on December 30.

Meanwhile, Stalin was pushing forward without mercy. On December 27, before a stunned audience, he announced the "liquidation of the kulak as a class." On January 30, 1930, he sent an order to "quickly liquidate counter-revolutionary kulak activists by confining them in concentration camps, not hesitating to carry out death sentences for organizers of terror acts, counter-revolutionary statements, and insurgent organizations."[163]

Open warfare broke out in the countryside as peasants refused to enter collective farms, and more than two million kulaks and their families were deported or imprisoned. The Gulag filled with peasants and anyone else who opposed Stalin. Discontent spread throughout cities. Grumbling from within Stalin's own ranks was heard from young party favorites, who had to be quickly expelled before further damage was done.[164] An outbreak of famine in Ukraine, southern Russia, and Kazakhstan claimed more than five million victims.

Demoted to a minor industrial post, Bukharin traveled through the Ukraine, where he saw children begging at train stations and famine everywhere. When he returned to Moscow, he collapsed, sobbing, on the couch in the Larin apartment. Anna's mother had to calm him down with valerian drops.[165]

Although he doubtless still harbored hopes that Stalin's policies would fail, Bukharin's political career as Lenin's "Golden Boy of the Revolution" had come to an end at age forty-one. He was relegated to the fringes of Soviet power as a candidate member of the

Central Committee. Having fallen from his lofty position as editor of *Pravda* and Politburo member, Bukharin busied himself in the Academy of Sciences and worked under Sergo Ordzhonikidze in his ministry of heavy industry. His best hope was for a quiet life out of the limelight.

CHAPTER 18

New Year's Eve, 1929:
Chastened Schoolboys Drop In on the Boss

THE FATEFUL YEAR 1929 ended badly for Bukharin, Tomskii, and Rykov. Only Rykov retained his job for the time being. Bukharin had been exiled to a minor industrial post. Attacks in the press continued, and he could not respond.

On New Year's Eve, Bukharin, Rykov, and Tomskii, who still lived in the Kremlin, appeared uninvited at Stalin's door. They came with a bottle of fine Georgian wine—an offering of peace and truce. Standing on the doorstep as Stalin opened the door, they wished him a new year of happiness and good health. He might well have sent his unexpected visitors away. His invited guests—Molotov and Mikoian—were already eating and drinking.

But again showing his cunning, Stalin heartily invited the newcomers in and bade them welcome. As they entered, they perhaps thought, Maybe we can mend things with Koba after all.[166]

CHAPTER 19

April 16, 1930:
Bukharin Sinks to His Knees

O N APRIL 14, 1930, the revered Russian poet Vladimir Mayakovsky committed suicide. Many interpreted the act as a protest against Stalin. Mayakovsky was friendly with Bukharin and, in fact, had earlier written a poem in praise of him. Bukharin had been the highest patron of arts and letters in the party. Mayakovsky's body lay in state at the Writers' Club, where all in attendance awaited the patron's visit with high anticipation.

Bukharin arrived, deposited his coat in a back room, and hastened to the conference room, where Mayakovsky's body lay in state. Bukharin stood for a long time in front of the casket. When the organizers finally asked him to speak, he paced back and forth. Then he hastily put his scarf and cap back on, looked at his hosts with his penetrating blue eyes, and said simply, "No." With that, he left through a side entrance.[167]

Bukharin's refusal to speak on such an occasion clearly showed that he was on his knees, trying to convince Stalin of his loyalty. Thereafter, he ostentatiously stopped seeing his former "rightist" comrades. He did not become a hermit—he appeared in the company of non-party scientists and writers—but gave up political contacts.

Some members of the so-called Bukharin school followed his example, cutting off relations with their teacher and one another. Others felt deserted: "We were all disappointed with Bukharin in that he gave up without warning us," one said later. "But we continued to love him."[168]

CHAPTER 20

July 1930:
With Anna in the Crimea

I N JUNE 1930, Nikolai Bukharin was diagnosed with a serious lung inflammation and ordered to the Crimea by his doctor. As delegates to the Sixteenth Party Congress arrived in Moscow at the end of the month, the ill and depressed Bukharin left the capital to become the Congress's most notable missing delegate. Also there, living in a party sanatorium with her ailing father, was Anna Larina, now sixteen years old. Bukharin took up residence in a dacha in a nearby town. Iurii Larin encouraged her to visit their friend, and Anna hitched a ride in order to do so. When she arrived, Bukharin was delighted to see her and said he'd had a premonition that she would come that day.

Although Bukharin was still involved in his uncomfortable relationship with Sasha Travina, he could no longer hold back his growing feelings for the young Anna. The two walked down a winding path to the sea. Neither brought up political subjects. Nikolai had brought with him a book of poems, from which he read aloud. One poem described a bedridden husband whose disease caused his hair to fall out, whereupon his wife cut off her tresses to be like him. Another concerned a man confined to a wheelchair; his wife poured acid over her face to even the score.

Bukharin asked Anna, "What do you think about a love like this?" Her answer: "Why make yourself ugly on purpose, turn yourself into a leper, throw acid in your face? Is it true that love requires this?"

Suddenly, looking at Anna sorrowfully and anxiously, he asked, "Would you be able to love a leper?" Flustered, Anna blurted out, "Do you mean love you?" He replied, "Yes," but added quickly that she should not answer because he feared what she'd say.

Returning to the dacha a day later, Anna found that Bukharin had gone out for a swim. When she arrived at the beach, she was told that he had not returned. The alarm was sounded and a rescue boat dispatched. Rescuers found him in a patrol vessel, under arrest for swimming in restricted waters. The coast-guard officers refused to believe that he was Nikolai Bukharin and comically demanded identification from a man clad only in swim trunks. A substantial crowd had gathered on the shore after hearing that Bukharin had disappeared. As he returned to shore, someone in the crowd shouted: "Nikolai Ivanovich, when will you stop playing pranks?" His answer: "When you stop calling me a rightist opportunist."

Bukharin's swimming escapade would later be used to confirm that he had feigned illness to skip the party congress—yet another addition to the long list of his purported sins against the party.

Returning to his dacha, Bukharin found a letter from Rykov wishing him a return to health and reporting that—despite Tomskii's removal from the Politburo—both men had conducted themselves with dignity at the congress. It was for the best, Rykov added, that Bukharin had not attended because he could not have maintained the "necessary calm."[169]

In fact, the party congress featured constant attacks on Rykov and Tomskii, as well as on the "truant" Bukharin. Even Lenin's widow, one of Bukharin's closest friends, was publicly humiliated for her failure to denounce Bukharin. Her mild condemnation was met with shouts from the crowd: "You are saying little. Say more! Completely unsatisfactory."[170]

Bukharin would have to wait four years until Anna agreed to marry him. The decision came as they stood and talked in front of the Union House on her twentieth birthday. The building, on Bolshaya

Dmitrovka Street not far from the Kremlin, was where Lenin's body had lain in state. Stalin would later choose it as the site of his three Moscow Show Trials. Both Bukharin and Anna passed by it regularly as they walked around central Moscow. Four years later, he would be condemned to death in this same building.

CHAPTER 21

October 14, 1930: Overtaken by "Insanities"

G ENRIKH IAGODA, the first head of the NKVD, was Stalin's right-hand man for collectivization. Yet he had the misfortune of being identified as a "rightist supporter" in the émigré press. No matter what he did, Iagoda could not shake Stalin's suspicions.

To convince Stalin of his loyalty, Iagoda went busily about fabricating cases of fantastic plots and conspiracies. One such fabrication from the fall of 1930 involved a fictional "underground party" that was planning such terrorist acts as the assassination of Stalin, allegedly with Bukharin's participation. The Master knew as well as Iagoda that the case was fabricated. Nevertheless, on October 14, he telephoned Bukharin to say he had evidence that Bukharin was trying to kill him.

In an understandably emotional response, Bukharin dashed off a letter to urgently request a meeting to refute this libelous assertion:

> After our telephone conversation, I am in a state of dismay. Not because you frightened me—you cannot frighten me and do not frighten me. But because your bizarre accusations clearly show you believe a diabolical, vile, and low provocation, which will lead to no good, as if you are destroying me politically as well as physically. My God, what kind of insanities are going on now?[171]

Although the letter bore the label "Strictly Personal," Stalin referred it to the Politburo. It was necessary, he told Bukharin, "to place the matter on record in the Central Committee in the hopes that it will find it possible to discuss the question."[172] Bukharin was called into the October 15 meeting of the Politburo and told that Comrade Stalin was correct in refusing to meet Bukharin to discuss this matter.

It is clear why Stalin wanted some shred of evidence in the record that Bukharin—as early as 1930—plotted his murder. The alleged plot was one of the charges on which Bukharin would later be convicted and executed.

CHAPTER 22

January 27, 1934:
Courtship, Bad Omens, and Marriage

IN THE TWO AND A HALF YEARS between the start of their courtship and their marriage, Anna Larina completed school, became a dedicated member of the party's youth league, and began her studies in the planning institute. After Nikolai's veiled confession of love in the Crimea, he and Anna continued to meet, attend concerts, read poetry, and take walks together. On Sundays, she sometimes accompanied him on hunts in the countryside. They often used public transportation, and passengers recognized him, declaring, "Hey, look. It's Bukharin, taking a ride!"

Anna felt that Nikolai was avoiding a serious conversation about a possible future together. Perhaps his reluctance was due to the great difference in their ages; the aftermath of his affair with Sasha Travina may also have played a role. Anna's mother considered their budding romance with skepticism, although her father took it with dead seriousness.

Many disagreements surfaced. Nikolai was jealous that Anna was seeing a student her own age. Once, when Nikolai saw them together, Anna's young suitor panicked and fled. The irate Bukharin told her in an imperious tone, "It is good that the era of duels has passed into history."

One evening in 1931, sitting opposite the Pushkin Memorial, Nikolai declared that they should either join their lives or part so that Anna could build her own life. Anna broke out in tears but gave no answer. They agreed to visit the opera the next evening.

When they arrived at her apartment, Bukharin slept on the couch while Anna spoke with her father, who admonished her: "Nikolai loves you very much. He is a sensitive emotional man, and if your feelings are not serious, you should leave him alone. Otherwise it might end badly for him."

Anna, alarmed, replied, "What do you mean, it might end badly for him? Not suicide?!" Larin said, "Not necessarily suicide, but he certainly does not need any extra worries."[173]

When Anna, the next day, left a note for Nikolai that she would have to cancel the opera because of a study group, he became convinced that she had spurned him. He refused to answer her calls, and only returned to her side after Iurii Larin contracted a fatal lung disease on New Year's Eve 1931.

As Iurii Larin lay on his deathbed, he imparted final words of advice to his daughter. He knew that if she married Bukharin, she would lead a troubled life. Their most telling conversation came on the morning of January 14, 1932. He would die later in the day. Larin asked Anna: "Do you still love Nikolai Ivanovich?" When she answered in the affirmative, she expected her father to tell her to forget him, but his answer, delivered in a barely audible tone, was profound:

"It would be more interesting to live ten years with Nikolai Ivanovich than your entire lifetime with another."[174]

As their courtship resumed, Nikolai and Anna attended concerts and lectures, and strolled through Moscow together. Nikolai often took her with him to events at the Academy of Sciences, the institution to which he often retreated after his political defeat. On one such occasion, he escorted Anna to a lecture by the renowned philosopher Anatoly Lunacharsky. She sat in the first row with luminaries of the arts and sciences.

After the event, Nikolai took her backstage to meet Lunacharsky, who had an interest in palmistry. As he examined the lines of her palm briefly but intently, his face darkened, and Anna barely caught his words: "A terrible fate awaits Anna Mikhailovna." When he noticed that Anna had heard, he tried to comfort her, saying, "Possibly the lines of your hand deceive me. That can happen."[175]

On the evening of Anna's twentieth birthday, in a chance encounter in front of the Union House, Nikolai added a grown-up element to their relationship—a straightforward invitation to make love: "Do you want me to come to your place right now?" When Anna answered in the affirmative, Nikolai responded: "But in that case, I will never leave you." Anna's response: "You don't have to."[176]

The lovers did not part again until three years later—when he was arrested.

CHAPTER 23

December 1, 1934:
Kirov Is Shot

O N DECEMBER 1, 1934, Politburo member and Leningrad party boss Sergei Kirov entered Leningrad party headquarters accompanied by his personal bodyguard and four other guards from the NKVD. Kirov had won the largest number of votes for reelection to the Central Committee at the 1934 party congress (the "Congress of Victors)"—a distinction that would not have sat well with Stalin. As he mounted the stairs, his bodyguard followed at a short distance, and the other four remained behind.

As Kirov reached the top step, a minor party official, known to have a vendetta against the party boss for a dalliance with his wife, fired a fatal shot through the back of his neck. The assassination of Kirov proved to be the starting point of Stalin's Great Terror. Over its course, almost a million persons, ranging from the party elite to ordinary citizens, would be executed.

Whether the murder of Kirov was the act of an aggrieved husband or a sinister plot devised by Stalin will never be clear. In any event, Stalin rushed to the scene, took charge of the investigation, and personally interrogated the assassin and eyewitnesses. The former supposedly committed suicide in his cell, and Kirov's bodyguard died in a suspicious automobile accident the very next day.

Stalin immediately used the incident to go after his political opponents. (Although politically neutered, he figured they might return.) The murder was for him a godsend. He could not hope to overcome the party's natural resistance to the execution of its own former leaders without a serious charge, such as assassination or espionage, and now he had one. Deviations from the unified party line justified removal from office, but nothing more drastic. If he could pin charges of murder on his opponents, capital punishment—on a sizable scale—would be within his grasp.

In Stalin's entourage scurrying to Leningrad was Genrikh Iagoda, who had to prove his mettle by following Stalin's order to "find the killers of Kirov among the followers of Zinovyev."[177] (Zinovyev, it should be remembered, was Trotsky's ally and Kamenev's compatriot.) When Iagoda failed to deliver evidence that Zinovyev and Kamenev were behind the murder, Stalin informed the Politburo that "Iagoda is clearly not up to the task."[178] His replacement was already in the wings: Nikolai Ezhov—ever faithful to Stalin and soon to be executioner of the Great Terror.

Kamenev and Zinovyev were first sentenced to prison in January 1935 for complicity in Kirov's murder. That did not satisfy Stalin. Nineteen months later, the two were again tried in the first Moscow Show Trial, along with fourteen other defendants. Each dutifully confessed to horrendous crimes.

Zinovyev admitted that "I am fully and completely guilty of having been an organizer of the Trotskyite-Zinovyevite bloc second only to Trotsky, the bloc which set for itself the aim of assassinating Stalin, Voroshilov, and a number of other leaders of the Party and the government. I plead guilty to having been the principal organizer of the assassination of Kirov."[179]

The Kamenev-Zinovyev trial allowed Stalin to hone his skills as an orchestrator of dramatic show trials. The defendants dutifully confessed in open court to espionage, murder, and mayhem after physical torture or empty promises that they or their families could live. Not only the defendants but also their spouses and adult children would be executed or imprisoned.

The executions of Kamenev and Zinovyev broke the taboo on imposing the death penalty for Bolshevik officials. Within the next two years, almost half of the Bolshevik elite would follow in their footsteps.

In their confessions, Kamenev and Zinovyev implicated Bukharin. The state prosecutor immediately announced an investigation.

CHAPTER 24

August 23, 1936:
Nadezhda Tries to Help

NIKOLAI BUKHARIN MARRIED HIS FIRST COUSIN, Nadezhda Lukina, in 1911 as he began his exile. They had been close friends since early childhood; they grew up together in quarters in the school where both their parents taught. Nadezhda, described only as beautiful with striking eyes, was one and a half years his senior. Nikolai and Nadezhda took up residence in a small apartment in Berlin. The young couple (he was twenty-three, she twenty-five) received money from both sets of parents back in Russia. Nikolai earned from his publications in socialist journals, and Nadezhda worked as a translator.

As Nadezhda's suffering from a degenerative spine disease intensified, they moved to Vienna (where they once entertained Lenin and his wife as visitors) in hopes of finding a cure. In the summer of 1915, her health further deteriorated, and they decided she should return to Moscow. With Lenin's assistance, Bukharin obtained a passport of a Jewish craftsman, Moise Dolgolevsky, for their travel to Stockholm via London.

Amid the war hysteria sweeping England, Bukharin and Lukina were arrested and jailed in Newcastle prison. Nadezhda's constant back pain made prison a torture. Released despite their false passports, the Bukharins traveled to Stockholm, and the ailing Nadezhda went on to Moscow, laden with revolutionary papers and brochures. They would not be reunited until after the October Revolution.[180]

When Nikolai Bukharin married his second wife, Esfir' Gurvich, in 1921, Nadezhda was devastated, but she and Nikolai continued to be close friends. In 1922, they traveled together to Germany for treatment. On their visa, they continued to be listed as husband and wife.

Nadezhda's deteriorating spinal condition eventually confined her to bed. When Anna spied her on a visit to a sanatorium in February 1932, she saw her as an "old woman sitting in a wicker chair and covered with a plaid blanket."[181] After her marriage to Bukharin, Anna and Nadezhda became friends, and she invited Nadezhda to live with them in their Kremlin apartment.

During the fateful events following Kirov's assassination, Nadezhda, now almost fully crippled, would drag herself from her room in the Bukharin Kremlin apartment to get the latest bad news. On August 21, 1936, when Anna learned that the state prosecutor had opened an investigation of Bukharin, Tomskii, and Rykov, Anna went into a state of shock. Her trauma intensified when she received news of Tomskii's suicide of the same day.

Kamenev's accusations prompted the indignant Nadezhda to swing into action in defense of her beleaguered former spouse. On August 23, she dispatched a letter to Stalin:

> Dear Iosif Vissarionovich (Stalin):
>
> I am writing you for the following reason. Being on Red Square on the day of Kirov's funeral, I saw that despicable scoundrel, Kamenev, greeting Comrade Mdivani with a smile of open *Schadenfreude*, which he suppressed immediately when he saw I was watching. It never would have entered my head that he was one of the guiding hands of the murder, but I saw that Comrade Kirov's death did not bother him.
>
> But I am troubled by another point: I did not see the face of Comrade Mdivani, because he stood with his back to me, but would Kamenev have displayed such an evil smile if he had not expected a similar reaction?

Nadezhda went on to advise Stalin that to check out Comrade Mdivani because "in a word, I was not able not to write you." (Her recommendation showed a sophisticated political sense: Mdivani was an old enemy of Stalin from his days in Georgia.) Nadezhda now came to the real reason for her letter—a defense of Bukharin:

You might ask why I am writing about Comrade Mdivani and not about N. I. Bukharin. I fully subscribe to the prosecutor's call for the most strict investigation because the most burdening accusations were leveled in the court. No matter how these criminal murderers with strange faces played their games, I do not doubt for one second the complete non-involvement of N. I. Bukharin with the Trotsky-Zinovyevite Center or in any kind of other criminal band.

With Communist Greetings

Devoted to you, as the only and great successor to Lenin, leading the country to a great victory.

N. M. Lukina (Bukharina)[182]

CHAPTER 25

April 25, 1935:
Humiliating Editor Bukharin

W HEN STALIN APPOINTED NIKOLAI BUKHARIN editor of the state
newspaper, *Izvestiia*, in the spring of 1934, the move was opti-
mistically interpreted as the Master relaxing as he basked in the
limelight of "successful" collectivization and industrialization. Any
hint of an actual relaxation would end with Kirov's assassination in
December.

Bukharin threw himself into his new work with characteristic
zeal, gathering around him leading journalists and writers. His
workday was full; he returned home at odd hours. Except on occasion after the birth of their son, he refused to take time off, even to
be fitted for a second suit that he needed for a trip abroad. The tai-
lor had to take measurements during an editorial meeting.[183]

Bukharin's editorship of *Izvestiia* served Stalin's purposes well.
The chief editor answered directly to the general secretary, and Stalin knew that Bukharin's fear of losing a prized position would keep
him in line. Moreover, the chief editor could be held responsible for
any ideological "deviations" of his writers. Stalin could humiliate
Bukharin by ordering him to print articles, in Stalin's crude expression, to "destruct" those out of favor.

Once Stalin chewed Bukharin out because the author of some
article, gushing with praise, had written that Stalin's mother called
him Soso. Demanded the irritated Master, "What's this 'Soso' business?"[184] In another case, Bukharin had to make an abject apology
to Molotov for misspelling his name ("Molokov," or "man of milk"):

"I ask your forgiveness for the annoying inexcusable blunder. We have punished those responsible."[185]

As editor of *Izvestiia*, Bukharin was also harassed by Stalin's henchman, Lev Mekhlis—Bukharin's successor as editor of *Pravda*—even for trivial transgressions. A March 1935 satirical article entitled "Almost Happy," by an *Izvestiia* correspondent with the byline of Comrade Zorich, landed Bukharin in trouble. The piece described in humorous terms the tribulations of petitioning the Moscow city government to build a small garage. A week later, an article entitled "Extortionary Impudence" appeared in *Pravda*, accusing Zorich of using the threat of an unfavorable article to blackmail the Moscow city government. *Pravda* claimed to possess a threatening letter to this effect written by Zorich's assistant.

In April 1935, the matter of Zorich's garage ended up before the Party Control Commission, the high-level agency responsible for the most important disciplinary cases.[186] The disciplinary hearing was attended by Bukharin, Mekhlis, Zorich, the head and deputy head of the Party Control Commission, and Bukharin's sole defender, Lenin's sister, Mariia Ul'ianova. Ludicrously, five top party and state officials had to set time aside to address Zorich's guilt and Bukharin's alleged negligence.

Bukharin defended Zorich as a "dedicated, honest, and thoughtful employee . . . distinguished by his modesty and . . . not the type of person to engage in tricks." The defense fell on deaf ears: "Don't cry for him Comrade Bukharin. We have a plaintiff. We are punishing him; you want us to feel sorry for him."

As the session proceeded, it became increasingly clear to Bukharin that the issue of the garage article was a setup. Mekhlis let it be known that Moscow party head Nikita Khrushchev himself had come to him "in exasperation." Allocating space for private garages, it seems, was a tough enough business without pressure from the press. That Khrushchev himself had been offended by a satirical piece in *Izvestiia* is unlikely. Stalin or Mekhlis probably brought the matter to his attention as a pretext to further discredit Bukharin.

After an hour of heated debate, the bureau decided to rebuke Comrade Zorich for his "gravest mistake in using *Izvestiia* for his personal interests." The "editorship" of *Izvestiia* (Bukharin) was also rebuked. The hearing ended on a bitter note, with the prosecuting official warning Bukharin. "Don't turn this case into a melodrama," to which the agitated editor retorted: "I fear that this matter will end up a tragedy."

The meeting ended with a stern rebuke of Bukharin by the head of the Party Control Commission, a Comrade Shkiriatov: "Are people really defended in this manner? Could you not have defended him in the proper way? Could you not have telephoned the head of the Moscow city council and decided the issue in this fashion?"

Bukharin's stubborn defense of the lowly Zorich showed his willingness to defend subordinates, but it would pay him little in return. As the criminal investigation of Bukharin intensified, it would be Bukharin's own colleagues who would break under torture and intimidation to give Stalin the "evidence" he needed to bring down Bukharin.

CHAPTER 26

March–April 1936:
Bukharin Opts to Stay and Fight

IN FEBRUARY 1936, Stalin commissioned Bukharin to lead a small delegation to negotiate the purchase of the Marx-Engels archive in France. Russian Menshevik émigrés were to serve as intermediaries. (Although the Mensheviks and Bolsheviks were once allies, Lenin's arrest order in the early days of Bolshevik rule sent most of them into exile.) Bukharin, Stalin said, could stay in Paris for as long as he needed—a mission that would bring him into regular contact with the sworn Menshevik enemies of the Bolshevik state.

Soviet officials unexpectedly granted Anna Larina permission to join him. She received her visa from Nikolai Ezhov, shortly to replace Iagoda, with the words: "Your beloved husband misses you; he can't live without his young wife." Anna arrived in Paris in early April. Obviously feeling the effects of late-term pregnancy, she fainted on the way to the Louvre. Still, she enjoyed Paris in spring, with its blooming chestnut trees, artists drawing sketches, and strolling lovers.

One of the highlights was a speech Bukharin gave at the Sorbonne. He was gratified that the venerable Austrian Marxist Rudolph Hilferding came to hear him. Bukharin was concerned what Moscow might think of their meeting, but "it wasn't my place, after all, to chase him away."

The trip posed risks. Bukharin would have to meet regularly with prominent Mensheviks, such as Fedor Dan and Boris Nicolaevsky. Stalin could accuse him of hatching anti-Soviet plots with them, and Bukharin would have no way of refuting the charges.

In allowing Bukharin and his pregnant wife to leave Russia and to meet with émigrés who would welcome him as a high-level defector, Stalin calculated that Bukharin would choose to return home. But he needed to give the friendly, voluble Bukharin time to make mistakes, to reveal "secrets" to his eager hosts, who would rush them into the émigré press. If Stalin miscalculated and Bukharin stayed abroad, he would be out of his reach.

Negotiations for the archive purchase proceeded slowly, thanks to Stalin's delaying tactics. After Stalin rejected one price after another, Bukharin's émigré counterpart noted: "You put a low price on Marx."[187]

What happened next will probably forever remain a mystery. Although Bukharin assured Larina that he was carefully avoiding being alone with the émigré negotiators, he appears to have told Menshevik leader Fedor Dan that Stalin was "a small, malicious man, no, not a man, a devil."[188] Strolling through Paris with the prominent French writer Andre Malraux, he said that Stalin "is going to kill me."

He may have confided most to his negotiating counterpart, Boris Nicolaevsky (also Rykov's brother-in-law). Nicolaevsky subsequently published an anonymous "Letter of an Old Bolshevik" in the Menshevik's *Sotsialistichesky Vestnik*,[189] describing the horrors of collectivization and dekulakization, and characterizing Stalin as a despot. The "Letter" would be used against Bukharin as proof that he conspired with foreign enemies. Only Bukharin, prosecutors would contend, could have disclosed this libelous information.

Bukharin's decision to return to Russia was extremely risky, for both him and Larina. When asked by one of the Mensheviks why he was doing so, Bukharin purportedly answered: "How could I *not* return? To become an émigré? No, I couldn't live as you, as an émigré." There was another consideration: although his wife was with him, Bukharin left behind in Moscow his father, his brother, his first wife, and his second wife and their daughter.[190]

Whether Bukharin should have anticipated what would happen if he returned home is uncertain. He presumably gained confidence and a sense of security from the fact that Stalin had appointed him editor of *Izvestiia* and treated him with occasional kindness or solicitude, creating a sense that perhaps bygones were indeed bygones.

Whatever the reason for returning to Stalin's Soviet Union, the decision cost Bukharin his life. And for Larina, it meant more than twenty years in the Gulag and exile.

CHAPTER 27

August 27, 1936:
What Accusers? They're Dead.

T HE YEAR 1936 began propitiously with the birth of a son, Iura. The forty-seven-year-old father was "cast into a state of joy." He was not only editor of *Izvestiia* but also a member of the Soviet Constitutional commission, which was drafting the "Stalin Constitution." Things appeared to be looking up.

As the summer approached, however, dark clouds were gathering. The Moscow trial of Kamenev and Zinovyev, on charges of murder and attempted assassination, was scheduled for mid-August. Although they would clearly be found guilty, execution seemed highly unlikely—no high Bolshevik official had been sentenced to the "highest measure of punishment." As the trial approached, Bukharin probably felt that he himself would not be touched. He had assiduously avoided contact with Kamenev and Zinovyev, as well as with his former allies.

But when Stalin awarded Bukharin a six-week vacation to visit remote Central Asia, he should have been suspicious of the timing. An avid alpinist, he left Moscow in early August to fulfill his dream of hiking in the Pamir Mountains of Uzbekistan. Stalin's plan was for Bukharin to miss entirely the tragic events that were soon to transpire in Moscow.

His sketchbooks and canvasses and a hunting rifle packed and ready, Bukharin and Larina followed the Russian custom of sitting silently for a moment in their dacha before he left for the airport. As he was driving off, his thirteen-year-old nephew ran after him, hysterically crying: "Uncle, do not go!" Bukharin calmed him: "I'll be back soon. You'll grow up, and we'll ride in the mountains together." As his wife watched the car depart, she could not have guessed that, as she later put it, soon "the joy of life would desert us."[191]

With Bukharin wandering the wilds of Uzbekistan, the trial of the Trotskyite United Center began on August 19, 1936. Kamenev and Zinovyev confessed to horrendous crimes, including the assassination of Kirov, the murders of writer Maksim Gorky and Politburo member Valerian Kuibyshev, and plots to murder Stalin and much of the Politburo. Their testimony was carried in the press, and as they started pointing fingers at Bukharin, Anna Larina became distraught.

On August 21, the state prosecutor announced an investigation of Bukharin, Rykov, and Tomskii. The next day, Tomskii committed suicide at his dacha, and three days after that, Kamenev and Zinovyev, along with twelve other defendants, were shot. Three of the major players in the "rightist-leftist" terrorist conspiracy were now dead.

Far away and out of contact, the unsuspecting Bukharin wrote two travelogue letters to his "Dear Koba," describing the region "as a whole kingdom of great importance which we are just now beginning to understand." His second letter, written on August 23, in the very midst of the dramatic events in Moscow, revealed that he was cutting short his trip due to the illness of a traveling companion.[192] Were it not for this illness, Bukharin would have returned to civilization—and the political moves being made against him—much later.

Bukharin resurfaced in a provincial Uzbek town on August 24, the day the death sentences of Kamenev and Zinovyev were announced. He also learned that they had implicated him as an accomplice. According to party rules, Bukharin had the right to confront his accusers face to face. He dashed off a frantic telegram to Stalin:

"To the Central Committee, Comrade Stalin: I just now read the defamatory testimony of the scoundrels. I am distressed to the depths of my soul. I am flying from Tashkent on the twenty-fifth. I ask you to pardon my interruption. 24/VIII. Bukharin."[193]

On his way to Tashkent, Bukharin, now a suspected enemy of the people, was put up in a government dacha. Uzbek party officials dared be in his presence only with witnesses on hand. At the dacha, the two accompanying Uzbek party officials showed Bukharin the latest newspapers on the trial, and one asked him whether he had heard that Tomskii had committed suicide. According to one account, the shocked Bukharin became physically ill upon learning this news.[194]

Back in the Kremlin, Larina feared that her husband had already been arrested but instead learned that he was arriving at the Moscow airport on the very day of Kamenev's and Zinovyev's scheduled execution. She herself reached the terminal late and found her husband, looking ill and distraught, slouched on a bench in the corner. He had wanted her to meet him at the airport because he thought he would be arrested there. On his shoulder hung decorative wool socks and a bell for Iura. Upon seeing his trusted chauffer, Bukharin cried out to him: "It's all a lie, and I will prove it."

The Bukharins decided to go directly to their Kremlin apartment, which had a direct telephone line to Stalin. As they entered the Kremlin through the Borovitskie gates, the guard let them pass without incident. (Said Bukharin to Larina: "He probably does not read the newspapers.")

He ran into the apartment, brushing aside the anxious questions of his elderly father, and began furiously dialing Stalin's number. A person with an unfamiliar voice answered and said that Stalin was not in Moscow. As Larina later bitterly observed, "Here was Nikolai Ivanovich seeking salvation from his own executioner."

That evening and the next day, Bukharin caught up on press accounts. To his dismay, letters were being published demanding his head. He dashed off a characteristically long missive setting forth his defense addressed to members of the Politburo and to state prosecutor Andrey Vyshinsky.

Bukharin's letter was a combination of outrage, self-pity, groveling, and abject flattery. It recounted his mad rush back to Moscow to learn that "my accusers have been shot, but their accusations live on" and said that he was distraught over the "shame and dishonor" of "resolutions that assume that my guilt has already been proven." He pleaded that, "I am not only not guilty of the offenses of which I have been charged, but I can say with pride that I have defended in recent years with all my enthusiasm and conviction the party line and the leadership of Stalin. Only a fool (or a traitor) could not understand the heroic accomplishments of the country, inspired and directed by the iron hand of Stalin."

Bukharin then went on to claim that he had had no contacts with the executed "traitors" other than brief encounters on minor matters (which he recounted in painful detail), and that he had broken off contact with Tomskii and Rykov in 1933. Bukharin showed no remorse over the fate of Kamenev and Zinovyev. "It is excellent that they shot the scoundrels. The air became immediately cleaner."

The appeal concluded: "I cannot endure living as I am now, with a heavy and deadly torment, when people fear to cross my path on the street, without there being any guilt on my side. I am so destroyed that I will sit in my apartment or dacha and will wait the call from the Central Committee or the prosecutor."[195]

When Bukharin departed for the wilds of Uzbekistan several weeks earlier, he hoped that he would be left alone. As a new father, he had gained a fresh lease on life—in the form of a young son, who he could raise together with a beautiful, devoted wife. His horror in Tashkent was twofold: one, the lifting of the ban on executions of the highest-level party officials; and two, the realization that the accusations of those "no longer among the living" would be enough to condemn him. His struggle for an accommodation that would give him a reasonable life had suddenly become a battle for his life.

CHAPTER 28

November 16, 1936: Bukharin Grovels

DESPITE THE CRIMINAL INVESTIGATION against him, Bukharin formally remained the editor of *Izvestiia*. He rarely visited the editorial offices, however, spending most of his time cooped up in his Kremlin apartment.

On November 16, 1936, he sent the following letter to "Comrade I. V. Stalin":[196]

Dear Koba:

Because I am not able (through no fault of my own) to write anything, and by my nature I simply cannot sit around as a passive, unfeeling dullard, I wrote in one of my sleepless nights this proposed poem. Without your approval, I will not show it to anyone on the [*Izvestiia*] editorial board, but if this work is deserving of attention, then I ask your permission to publish it. . . .

If you approve this and consider that it should be published under my name, then I would of course be happy to do so. If you find, contrary to expectations, that it is not appropriate, then I will not make any effort to use this new poetic genre.

Your deeply devoted, N. Bukharin

Bukharin attached his "Poem About Stalin" (in seven odes), the last lines of which read:

Amidst a troop of millions, amid armies, amid heroes,
Stands our Stalin, our beloved commander,
Ready to soar on wings to the sun of battles,
Trumpets sound of the times. And the loud cry resounds:
"Lead us in the new battle, now that the enemy attacks!"

And he wisely looks into the distance, with a searching gaze
On the army of the enemy. The Great Stalin.

To a leadership that was accustomed to interpreting subtle hints about whether someone was or was not in the Master's favor, Bukharin's poem was a failed attempt to extract a positive signal. Stalin was not taken in, and with good reason: if the poem had been published under Bukharin's name, it would have meant that Bukharin was in fact back in Stalin's favor.

CHAPTER 29

December 4, 1936:
Dress Rehearsal for Arrest

BUKHARIN'S WAIT FOR A CHANCE to rebut the charges against him turned out to be four months. Finally, on December 4, 1936, he was called to a hostile Central Committee plenum. The session dealt officially with the expulsion of two party officials: Iurii Piatakov, deputy minister of heavy industry, the Piatakov so highly praised by Lenin; and Bukharin's childhood friend, Grigorii Sokol'nikov, the eyewitness to the fateful Kamenev-Bukharin meeting of July 1928.

Both were accused of assassinations and other terrorist acts along with the destruction of Soviet industry. They were shortly to be the main defendants in the Second Moscow Show Trial in January 1937. Piatakov would be executed; Sokol'nikov would be sentenced to prison, where he would be murdered by the NKVD.[197]

The one-day plenum began with the new NKVD head, Nikolai Ezhov, reading the indictment against Piatakov and Sokol'nikov. The one hundred fifty-two delegates (not counting invited guests) listened as Ezhov ticked off Piatakov's and Sokol'nikov's plans to kill the "main leaders of our party and state."[198] As Ezhov droned on, a voice from the hall interrupted with impatience: "What about Bukharin?" provoking agitation in the hall.[199]

With this prompting, Ezhov turned to Bukharin. He quoted from Sokol'nikov's confession the allegation that the "rightists" had joined their bloc, that they had accepted a joint platform (named after an obscure regional party secretary, Martem'ian Riutin, its purported author), and that Bukharin had had a conspiratorial meeting with

Kamenev again in 1932. As these revelations were uttered, shouts of "Rascals!" and "Villains!" filled the Kremlin's Sverdlov Hall.[200]

At this point, Stalin made a rare interjection: "I must say that Bukharin, Tomskii, and Rykov denied that they had a platform. There was indeed a platform, but they were not at ease to disclose it, and they hid it. Its goal was to re-establish private capital and to open the way for foreign capital—"

> BERIIA (interrupting): Such good-for-nothings!
>
> STALIN:—to re-establish private capital in agriculture, cut back collective farms, and re-establish kulaks.

Ezhov then continued his statement: "Insofar as the names of rightists were mentioned during interrogations, I and Comrade Kaganovich arranged confrontations according to instructions from the Central Committee [namely Stalin] for Comrades Bukharin and Rykov with Sokol'nikov and Piatakov. It is true that the results were not very concrete, but in any case, they allowed a judgment to form that, without doubt, the rightists were informed about all these terrorist and other plans of the Trotsky-Zinovyev bloc."

> BUKHARIN (rushing to the podium): Allow me, allow me to speak!
>
> EZHOV (brushing him off): Accusations come not only from the accused but also from within rightist circles, such as a Comrade Sosnovskii and other Bukharin associates at *Izvestiia*.
>
> BERIIA: Who is Sosnovskii?
>
> EZHOV: He is a noted journalist, lately working at *Izvestiia*. Sosnovskii related that, in a conversation, Bukharin said: "Let's take the Riutin Platform, which from the first to the last line—
>
> (Bukharin tries to interrupt.)
>
> EZHOV:—does not contain the word "terror," but this is not necessary. It is evident from the context.
>
> MIKOIAN: When was this conversation?
>
> EZHOV: In 1935 or 1936.

Such references to Bukharin's anti-party activities after 1929 were particularly damaging to Bukharin, who freely admitted his earlier "sins" but swore that he had been faithful to the party ever since.

After citing incriminating testimony from other Bukharin associates, Ezhov concluded: "This is the testimony we have from those who have been executed [Kamenev and Zinovyev], the heads of the Parallel Center [Piatakov, Sokol'nikov], and the testimony of members of rightist organizations. . . . When we arranged the confrontations, there was no doubt that the rightists were informed about these terrorist activities; they knew the Trotskyites had gone over to terror. They were not only informed; they sympathized."

Bukharin took the floor, and he appeared to have expected to be arrested: "It may be that I am speaking for the last time before you."[201] He began by referring to Piatakov and Sokol'nikov as "scoundrels" and praised the NKVD for its vigilance.

> **BERIIA** (cutting off those ingratiating remarks): Better you tell us about your participation in this matter. Tell us what you did.
>
> **BUKHARIN:** I will tell all. . . . It is difficult for me to speak because there has been a mass of letters, people, tears, and gestures, and all of these have been lies.

Bukharin began his defense by claiming that Kaganovich, who was present at his confrontation with Sokol'nikov, concluded that he was not incriminated and instructed the prosecutor to close the Bukharin case. Bukharin: "So why is this matter being brought up again?"

> **KAGANOVICH** (in a jumble of doubletalk): We were then talking about juridical matters. One matter is juridical, the other is political.
>
> **BUKHARIN:** For God's sake, don't interrupt. I asked that it be confirmed that Sokol'nikov did not conduct any political talks with me. Moreover, in the confrontation, Ezhov specially asked me not to mention that Tomskii was already shot or that they were all [Kamenev and Zinovyev] shot.
>
> **VOICE:** Tomskii shot himself and was not shot. (Bukharin later went back and corrected the text to say "shot himself.")
>
> **BUKHARIN:** Whatever. He already did not exist. What did the confrontation with Sokol'nikov yield? There was not one word about politics, and suddenly this horrible, monstrous accusation! On this basis, there was formed the "impression" [Bukharin himself added quotation marks] that I participated in this business.
>
> **VOICE:** But did you read the testimony of Uglanov[202] and Kulikov[203] [two of his former allies]?
>
> **BUKHARIN** (avoiding the question, wishing to deal with one accuser at a time): I already wrote several times about Sosnovskii; comrades, why did you not arrange a confrontation with him? I did not have

one conversation with him relating to politics and never spoke about the Riutin platform. I did not read the Riutin platform, because it was shown to me only one time by order of Comrade Stalin. I did not see it nor was I informed about it until that time.

STALIN: We offered you a confrontation with Sosnovskii, but you were sick. We looked for you.

BUKHARIN: I wrote to Ezhov that I would drag myself in sick, but no one called me.

MOLOTOV: In any case, this business does not depend—

BUKHARIN (interrupting): But the plenum is now. Why not hold the confrontation now? Comrades, I must tell you that I never denied that I led an oppositional battle against the party in 1928 and 1929. But I do not know how to convince you that I knew absolutely nothing about these plans, platforms, or goals! Can you believe that I am that kind of person? Can you really believe that I could have something in common with these diversionaries, wreckers, and scoundrels after thirty years in the party? Truly, this is something insane!

MOLOTOV: Kamenev and Zinovyev were also in the party their entire lives.

BUKHARIN: Kamenev and Zinovyev wanted power, and they sought power. Did I strive for power? There are a number of old comrades who know me well, not only from platforms but know my soul—

BERIIA (interrupting): It is hard to know the soul.

BUKHARIN: Yes, it is difficult to know the soul, but you are judging the person. How can you make such accusations without allowing me confrontations with all my accusers?

BERIIA: They will do this.

BUKHARIN: Good, Comrade Beriia. I did not ask you. I am speaking about something that does not depend on you.[204]

The desperate Bukharin then turned to another line of argument: "Why should the party's enemies not try to harm the party from within? Why should they not try to sink, to destroy honest people? Why not, tell me?" (Restless movement in the hall).[205]

Hoping this point had sunk in, Bukharin launched into a self-serving account of defending Stalin against the "vile manner" in which Nobel Prize–winning scientist Ivan Pavlov spoke about Stalin. The unimpressed Molotov asked, "What does this have to do with the accusations against you?"

BUKHARIN: Why would I have defended Stalin if I am a wrecker, if I hate Comrade Stalin, whom I in fact love, if I hate the leadership of the party, which I in fact love, and if I sinned earlier against the party for which I am prepared to die? [Recognizing that he had gotten carried away, Bukharin later edited out "being ready to die."] Life is not so dear to me, this has all worn me out to such a degree, but I want back my political honor! (Movement and skeptical laughter in the hall).[206]

Bukharin's complaint that he was not allowed a confrontation with Kamenev and Zinovyev before they were executed prompted Stalin to step in to explain why:

STALIN: You see, the impression was formed that there was no basis for your indictment. But doubts of a party character remained. It seemed to us that Rykov and Tomskii for sure, and maybe Bukharin, could not have not known that the scoundrels, Kamenev and Zinovyev, were preparing evil deeds, but they did not tell us.

VOICE: That is a fact.

BUKHARIN (to Stalin): Do you have no conscience?

STALIN: I am only saying this because it seemed to us that we had little to go on to turn you over to the courts.

BUKHARIN: Comrade Stalin, is it not true that as soon as I learned by chance about Kamenev's and Zinovyev's accusation, I, finding myself in the middle of nowhere, got on a plane and sent you a telegram? Comrade Stalin, I considered it completely elementary that I should have had a confrontation with them.

STALIN: I told them not to touch Bukharin, but to wait.

BUKHARIN: I think we need to judge according to results. . . . I was late by a few hours. Was it not possible to wait a little while [with the executions] to allow me a confrontation? The matter is not about mercy, but about political honor. [207]

To this point, Bukharin appeared to be holding his own, but his defense crumbled when confronted with the long list of friends and associates who had incriminated him. Stalin came to the heart of the matter in his low-key, methodical manner: "Even though there are thousands of testimonies against you, you are not distressed. You say wait, we'll explain it all, but when we have accusations of such a person as Kulikov . . . He is regarded as an honest person, is he not?"

BUKHARIN: I have not seen Kulikov since 1929.

STALIN: When there are accusations of persons such as Kulikov, Uglanov, Sosnovskii . . . Why should they all lie to us about you? They can lie but why? Can we hide this fact? You are disturbed that we have placed this question before the plenum, but you must answer here before this fact.

BUKHARIN: I am not disturbed that this question was placed before the plenum but that Ezhov reaches the conclusion that I knew about terror, that I am guilty of terror, and so forth. With respect to Kulikov, it is very simple. We must determine where and when he met with me, because he has not seen me since 1929.

STALIN: This is possible to find out.

The fact that Stalin and Ezhov had lined up so many accusations is testimony to the power and efficiency of the NKVD. In his exchange with Bukharin, Stalin got from Bukharin a clear statement that he had not seen Kulikov since 1929. Bukharin's "lie" would come back to haunt him, and Stalin already knew it would.

Before being turned over to Stalin's cronies for further questioning, Bukharin underscored the predicament he was in: "It is simple. If you say I met with this person, you say it was for tactical reasons. If you say I did not meet this person, aha, this means I did not meet with him for conspiratorial reasons. Whether it is Friday or Saturday, I am in any case a son of a bitch. Either I am absolutely 100 percent a son of a bitch or everything else falls away as something that cannot be believed."[208]

Molotov's turn came next. He warned delegates not to be swayed by "Bukharin's tears and wavering voice." He then went on to list all of Bukharin's friends and colleagues who had been exposed as enemies: "I do not understand how it is possible to swim in such a milieu and not to feel that something is wrong. This speaks at a minimum about a lack of Bolshevik sensitivity, that a person could not distinguish an enemy from a friend."[209]

Stalin's deputy, Lazar Kaganovich, was the last of a long list of speakers before Stalin's summation. He, as a witness to the confrontation between Bukharin and Sokol'nikov, made the most devastating charge: "I think that we can clearly say that you had your own organization. It was set up to have its own army, carry out its own plans, including terrorist acts and executions."

BUKHARIN (aghast): What are you talking about? You've gone out of your mind, Comrade Kaganovich![210]

The session ended with Stalin's instruction to deal with Bukharin and Rykov at the next plenum, scheduled for March 1937. "It is very painful," Stalin declared, "to speak of the past crimes of comrades as authoritative as Bukharin and Rykov. Therefore we will not hurry with the decision, comrades, but continue the investigation. We must consider the case unresolved."[211]

A commission headed by Mikoian was appointed to report to the next plenum.

Stalin ended with a warning to Bukharin not to follow Tomskii's path of suicide: That, Stalin declared, "is one of the very last, sharpest, and easiest means, which before death, before leaving this world, to spit a final time on the party, to deceive the party. And this, Comrade Bukharin, is the hidden motive of the latest suicides. And you, Comrade Bukharin, want us to believe your word?"

> BUKHARIN: No, I do not want this [suicide].
> STALIN: Never and under no circumstances?
> BUKHARIN: No, I do not want that.[212]

Stalin needed Bukharin as the star witness in his final Moscow Show Trial, and suicide would obviously destroy that plan. Stalin therefore kept holding out hope to Bukharin: maybe all these accusations are mistakes, but we need you around to convince us.

CHAPTER 30

December 1936–January 1937: Confrontations

AFTER THE DECEMBER 4 PLENUM, Bukharin spent the next three months shuttered in a small room in his Kremlin apartment. Ironically, it was Stalin's former bedroom, the very place in which Stalin's wife, Nadezhda, committed suicide. Bukharin lamented: "Nadia died here. So will I."[213]

The room had a small sink and toilet, and Nikolai scarcely left it. NKVD couriers brought the incriminating testimonies of associates and friends to his door. As he read them, he remarked: "If I were someone unknown to myself, I would believe it all." He left the apartment only to attend confrontations with his accusers.

Bukharin, despite all, continued to cling to a thread of hope, even while whispering to Anna, "Could it be that Koba has lost his mind?"[214] Frantically dispatched long letters to the Master to rebut the slanders produced no replies. Anna noticed that Bukharin was growing thin and old, his red hair turning gray.

Save when tending to their child, she was constantly at her husband's side. On one occasion, she returned to see him with a revolver in his right hand and his left supporting his head. In response to her frightened scream, he said that he was not able to do it yet, and that in any case it should not happen in her presence.[215]

At the end of December, a courier delivered a package with five seals containing the testimony of Karl Radek, his close friend of twenty years, who testified that Bukharin was involved in various terrorist activities. Bukharin and Radek had been youthful allies in exile before the revolution. They worked together closely in the Comintern, and Radek was a chief correspondent under Bukharin for *Izvestiia*.

Bukharin's one-word reaction to Radek's testimony: "awful!" He was especially bitter because he had intervened twice on Radek's behalf when the latter was arrested and imprisoned. He would later tell the Central Committee that he had "spent sleepless nights thinking whether I should have done this. . . . But should I turn into such a coward that I am not ready to take such a risk?"[216]

Summoned to a confrontation with Radek on January 13, 1937, Bukharin hoped he could persuade Radek to retract his testimony.[217] One can imagine the mood as the old friends confronted each other under the watchful eyes of virtually the entire Politburo. Bukharin came to the meeting from his Kremlin apartment; Radek was brought in from his prison cell.

Ezhov, who was presiding, began by asking Radek to summarize his charges. Radek testified that he was instructed to be Bukharin's contact person with the Trotskyites after Bukharin assumed the *Izvestiia* editorship in the spring of 1934. It was not until summer that they had a direct discussion about their "insane situations" as leaders in the leftist and rightist blocs.

Bukharin told him, Radek testified, that "our attitude is the same as yours, an attitude in favor of terror" and that he, Rykov, and Tomskii were the leaders of the rightists. Radek added that he did not need to tell Bukharin who led the Left because Bukharin "had already been in contact with Piatakov" on that subject.

Bukharin periodically interrupted Radek's testimony with gasps of disbelief: "I do not understand why you have to make all this up and lie!" After one such outburst, Radek retorted: "I also screamed when Sokol'nikov and Putna spoke against me in our confrontations. When I returned home, I said to myself: they are the world's greatest villains."

Stalin then moved to place on the record that Radek's testimony was given voluntarily: "In your testimony, you described a number of meetings with Bukharin in 1934, when Bukharin, as you say, spoke about the perspective for the destruction of the USSR in war, about a bloc with the rightists, and that this destruction would be the best way to power. Did you say this voluntarily?

RADEK: Yes, completely voluntarily. I would not guarantee that Bukharin said "the best way"; maybe he said something like "the most realistic way."

When Radek testified that Bukharin had told him that he accepted the purported rightist agenda (the Riutin Platform), Bukharin saw an opening. This could not have happened because both wives were present that evening. Radek's explanation was disarmingly simple: "Because I did not want to involve either wife, after they arrived at our apartment, I said to Anna that my wife is preparing dinner, and perhaps you wish to help. We were left alone and spoke quickly."

In concluding his testimony, Radek affirmed his main accusations: Bukharin knew about the policy of terror, sabotage of industry, concessions to the Germans, and Trotsky's contacts with them. He also knew who headed the leftists.

EZHOV (turning to Bukharin): Do you deny this?
BUKHARIN: Every word!

Unprompted, Radek reaffirmed that his testimony was not coerced. "I am obliged to say that no one forced me to say what I said. No one threatened me before I gave my testimony. I was not told that I would be shot if I refused. Besides that, I am sufficiently grown up to not believe any promises made to me in prison."

Radek, perhaps as a reward for his "services," was sentenced to ten years of penal labor, one of the few "conspirators" who escaped the death sentence. He was killed in a labor camp in 1939, under the direct orders of the NKVD's Beriia.[218] He was too dangerous to have around, even within the confines of a labor camp.

Radek's testimony in the presence of Politburo members struck a devastating blow to Bukharin's defense. Given their long association, Radek's account sounded a chord of presumed truth. Bukharin would surely have been tempted to join forces with Stalin's other opponents. It would be natural for him to hope for the failure of

Stalin's policies that would result in his being "removed." All of that would ring true to even a doubting member of the Politburo.

Bukharin's January 13 confrontation with Radek contrasted sharply with another one, 10 days later, with Iurii Piatakov, the former deputy minister of heavy industry and Bukharin's earlier alleged contact with Trotsky. If Bukharin had been puzzled by Radek's behavior, there was no doubt as to why Piatakov had testified that Bukharin was part of a huge conspiracy to unseat Stalin. Upon returning to his apartment, Bukharin told Anna that Piatakov looked "like a walking corpse," like "Piatakov's shadow, a skeleton with its teeth knocked out."[219]

The broken Piatakov paused when Bukharin asked him why he testified falsely. His boss, industry czar and Politburo member Sergo Ordzhonikidze, distressed by Piatakov's appearance, bent over him to ask, "Can your testimony really be voluntary?" After Piatakov nodded in the affirmative, Ordzhonikidze pressed further: "Absolutely voluntary?" Piatakov did not reply.

Piatakov had one week to live: he was executed on January 30. At his trial, the iron-willed Bolshevik managed to discredit his own confession, saying, "Any punishment you inflict will be easier than the very fact of this confession."[220] In less than three weeks, the independent and inquisitive Sergo Ordzhonikidze would also be dead, another likely suicide.

CHAPTER 31

February 15, 1937:
"I Will Begin a Hunger Strike"

NIKOLAI BUKHARIN'S doorbell rang on February 14, 1937, and an NKVD officer delivered a packet of materials announcing a Central Committee plenum five days hence. The first agenda item was "The Question of N. I. Bukharin and A. I. Rykov." Ominously, "Comrade" was not placed before their names. Bukharin had already dispatched a hundred-page declaration refuting the charges against him. Now he sat down at his desk to pen another response:

> I am not able to live. I already answered my accusers. I am in no condition physically or morally to come to the plenum. I am not able to walk. I am not able to endure the atmosphere. I am in no condition to speak. I do not want to wail, to fall into hysterics, or to faint as my own people defame and libel me.
>
> My written defense should be read out loud, and I ask you to distribute it. In this situation when I, being with my whole heart with you, am to be regarded by many as a turncoat and enemy, I have only two options—to either be rehabilitated or to depart from the scene. In this extraordinary situation, I will begin a hunger strike as long as these accusations of treachery, wrecking, and terrorism are not withdrawn.
>
> I will not live with such accusations. So that there is not the appearance of struggle with you, comrades, I will not tell anyone else. I will also not use other means of struggle. My hunger strike is directed against my accusers.

Bukharin ended his declaration with a final plea. "My last wish: Tell my wife about the plenum's decision. Let me, if I am convicted to go to the end of this road of sorrows, die here."[221]

Stalin anticipated that Bukharin would try some desperate form of resistance. He had to somehow coax him to attend. The announcement of a hunger strike still lay unsent as two men entered the Bukharins' Kremlin apartment displaying eviction orders. Just then, the phone rang. It was Stalin, playing his psychological games, asking solicitously how things were going. When told about the ongoing eviction, Stalin loudly ordered the men to go away. The episode reminded Bukharin that he, Stalin, could put his family out on the street at any time.

After the men left, Bukharin dashed into the storage closet, began writhing on the floor, and cried out that he should have foreseen what would happen, should not have loved Anna, and should not have had a child with her. That evening, she sent his declaration of a hunger strike to the Central Committee.

Two days into his defiant act, Bukharin already looked ashen, with sunken cheeks and hollow eyes. He refused all nourishment except water, and angrily shattered a glass of water into which his wife tried to smuggle some orange juice.

The plenum, scheduled to begin on February 19, was postponed until the 23rd. Cause of the delay: the untimely death of Sergo Ordzhonikidze, a likely suicide covered up as a heart attack. The revised schedule now included a third point: "The question of N. I. Bukharin's anti-Party behavior in regard to the hunger strike he has announced to the plenum." Somehow interpreting the added item as a positive sign, Bukharin decided to attend after all. Maybe Stalin would let him off with a light punishment!

On the day of the plenum, after days of fasting, Bukharin was so weak that he had to practice walking around the apartment. Anna helped him walk the short distance to Sverdlov Hall, on the snowy night of February 23, not knowing if she would ever see him again.

Upon entering the ornately domed Sverdlov Hall, the 125 delegates, 57 Control Commission members, and 51 invited guests signed attendance sheets next to their printed names. The names of those already purged were left standing, perhaps as a reminder to the others to take care. As Bukharin entered, they all seemed to avert their glances. His co-defendant, Aleksei Rykov, rushed to him, took him aside, and whispered that Tomskii—with his suicide—"proved to be the most farsighted of us." Unable to walk to his seat, Bukharin sank to the floor of the isle. Stalin walked over to him and asked:

"So who did you tell about your hunger strike, Nikolai—the party, the Central Committee? Just look at yourself, you've wasted away to nothing. Ask the plenum to forgive you for your hunger strike." Bukharin gathered his strength to ask why he should do that if he is to be expelled anyway.

Stalin responded reassuringly, within earshot of delegates: "No one is going to expel you from the party."[222] Nearby delegates urged him on: "Come, come, Nikolai, ask forgiveness from the plenum. You did a bad thing."[223] Bukharin had already given up one bargaining chip by even appearing. He was now asked to give up his final chip "for the sake of the party."

The evening session began with a long indictment read by Ezhov.[224] Following that, Anastas Mikoian addressed Bukharin's hunger strike. He equated it with Trotsky's street demonstrations before his expulsion, but said that because Bukharin had no followers, he had to invent a "new weapon" to "threaten" the Central Committee: "I do not know how a member of the party, a Bolshevik, can write such words to the Central Committee? Bukharin has declared a naked ultimatum instead of a request to discuss these issues, instead of coming and declaring that 'I made mistakes, I ask forgiveness.'"[225]

When Bukharin's time finally came, he answered Mikoian's charges in a despondent mood but a defiant manner: "I first want to say that I know the Central Committee well enough to immediately rule out that it can be frightened by anything."[226] That was a veiled reference to Stalin who in fact *was* the committee.

VOICE: Then why did you write that you'll not stop your hunger strike until the charges are dropped?

BUKHARIN: Comrades, I plead with you not to interrupt because it is very difficult for me, simply difficult physically, to speak. I'll answer any question, but do not interrupt me now. In my letter I described my psychological condition. I did not refer to the Central Committee because it, as such, has not accused me officially. I have been accused by the press, not by the Central Committee. I described my condition as it should be understood as a person. If, of course, I am not a human being, then there is nothing to understand. But I consider myself a human being and that I have the right to write about my psychological condition in this particularly difficult moment of my life. And in this regard, there was no attempt to frighten or deliver ultimatums.

STALIN: And your hunger strike?

BUKHARIN: And I'll continue my hunger strike. I told you, wrote to you, because I, in despair, grasped at this option. I wrote to a narrow circle because, with such accusations hanging over me, it is impossible to live. I am not able to shoot myself because then they'll say that I committed suicide to harm the party; but if I die, as from a disease, what would you lose from this?

VOICE: Blackmail!

ANOTHER VOICE: A base trick. Curse that tongue of yours. You should think about what you say!

BUKHARIN: But understand how difficult it is for me to live.

STALIN: And is it easy for us?

BUKHARIN: It is easy for you to speak about me. What have you to lose, especially if I am a son of a bitch, a wrecker, etc. Why should anyone be sorry? I have no pretensions. I describe what I think, and I live on. If this is associated with some tiny political cost, I would without doubt carry out all that you ask [laughter]. Why are you laughing? There is absolutely nothing funny here.

Bukharin returned home after the grueling session. He told Anna of Stalin's promise of leniency—"No one is going to expel you"—and he ate a bit of food for the first time in a week. He slept fitfully, imagining that someone was banging on the wall from the apartment of the deceased Ordzhonikidze. He returned to the plenum in a miserable state the next evening.[227]

Bukharin began the February 24 session with a brief announcement: "I ask the plenum of the Central Committee to forgive my ill-advised and politically harmful act of declaring a hunger strike."[228]

STALIN: You are admitting little!

BUKHARIN: I can explain my declaration more clearly. I ask the plenum to accept my apology because I did indeed place the plenum under an ultimatum by my unusual move.

KAGANOVICH: An anti-Soviet move.

STALIN (ignoring Kaganovich): Which is to excuse and pardon.

BUKHARIN: Yes, yes and pardon.

STALIN: Yes, yes.

MOLOTOV: You agree that your so-called hunger strike can be considered by our comrades as an anti-Soviet act?

VOICE: Yes, that is it. Bukharin must say so.

BUKHARIN: If some comrades view it in this way. (Noise in the hall.)

VOICES: And how otherwise?

BUKHARIN: But, comrades, this did not enter my subjective intention.

VOICE: But this is how it was perceived.

BUKHARIN (in effect admitting defeat): Of course, this further deepens my guilt. I ask the Central Committee again to forgive me.

Stalin now had Bukharin at his complete mercy. First, the resolute Bukharin was not going to attend the plenum, but he dutifully showed up. Second, the defiant Bukharin was not going to stop his hunger strike until the charges were dropped. Now he was admitting to "anti-Soviet blackmail." He had transformed himself from an object of pity into one of ridicule.

As the evening session proceeded, Bukharin's hunger strike became a joke as delegate after delegate savaged Bukharin. The wisecracking began with an exchange between Molotov and Stalin:[229]

MOLOTOV: Only two days passed since Bukharin declared a hunger strike, and he came here and declared: "I have not eaten for four days." He should have read his own letter. Bukharin is a comedian, an actor—a small provincial actor. This hunger strike is the act of an insignificant actor. Did true revolutionaries carry out hunger strikes in this fashion? This is the act of a counter-revolutionary, Bukharin.

STALIN: We don't have a count. How many days has he fasted?

MOLOTOV: He said that the first day he fasted 40 days and 40 nights, the second day 40 days and 40 nights, and then every day thereafter 40 days and 40 nights.

STALIN: Why did he begin his hunger strike at midnight?

MOLOTOV: I think because people do not eat at night; their doctors do not recommend it.

Bantering about the hunger strike became a running theme as the various Politburo members and Central Committee delegates lined up to attack Bukharin:

DELEGATE (SEMON BUDENNYI): Bukharin never even began a hunger strike. He only said that he fasted from midnight to morning, that is, he was on a hunger strike the entire night. (Laughter.)[230]

Bukharin's agreement to appear before the delegates and to abandon his hunger strike left him with no remaining defenses. He spent the rest of the plenum reeling from blows from all directions, like a defeated prizefighter when the referee refuses to halt the bout.

CHAPTER 32

February 24, 1937:
To a Future Generation

AFTER THE SECOND SESSION of the February Central Committee plenum, Bukharin realized that all hope was lost. He knew that he would soon be arrested and probably executed. Yet, according to Anna, he became more collected: "Giving up hope for vindication in his lifetime, he turned to posterity." He sat down and composed a declaration of innocence and a request to be reinstated in the party by a future generation of party leaders. Bukharin seemed confident that Anna would survive the trials and tribulations that lay ahead and would live to deliver his declaration.

Knowing that a written declaration would not be safe, Bukharin got Anna to repeat it over and over until he was convinced that she knew it. Then he destroyed the text. In prison, Anna would begin her day reciting to herself her late husband's last testament:[231]

> To a Future Generation of Party Leaders,
>   In what may be the final days of my life, I am certain that sooner or later the filter of history will inevitably wash the filth from my head. I never was a traitor; I would have unhesitatingly traded my own life for Lenin's; I loved Kirov, and never undertook anything against Stalin. I ask the new young generation of Party leaders to read my letter aloud at a plenum of the Central Committee, to vindicate me and to reinstate me in the Party.[232]

Anna Larina would indeed survive to deliver Bukharin's declaration to the party's "future generation." But not until the party was in its last years of existence would it be led by leaders sufficiently disenchanted with the system to be receptive to his message.

CHAPTER 33

February 24–25, 1937: On the Whipping Post

WITH THE SIDESHOW of Bukharin's hunger strike out of the way, Molotov called the plenum back into session to discuss "the Case of Comrades Bukharin and Rykov." The evening session began with a fifteen-minute indictment read in an incongruous baritone voice by the dwarf-like Ezhov.[233]

The indictment revealed the fruits of his three-month investigation. In the December plenum, Bukharin was only charged with being an organizer of the anti-Soviet rightist organization and knowing about and sympathizing with the Trotsky-Zinovyev bloc's planned use of terror. On these points, Ezhov now asserted, the guilt of Bukharin was established beyond a shadow of a doubt. He was about to reveal far more serious crimes.

Ezhov walked his audience through a confusing maze of names, places, and clandestine meetings in apartments, in dachas, and on street corners, where Bukharin and his allies allegedly planned their evil deeds. Although Bukharin and his rightists had agreed to cease their factional opposition, they actually went underground, adopted a secret opposition platform, and planned "acts of individual terror" to remove Stalin and his regime. They had a "holy hatred" of Stalin and, as early as 1928, openly talked about his assassination. Ezhov charged that at the start of 1933, Bukharin personally ordered the assassination of Stalin. As in ancient Rome: "The appearance of a Caesar inevitably brings about the appearance of a Brutus."[234]

Ezhov assured the delegates that "The investigation of the rightists was carried out with care and objectivity as confirmed by the fact that before different investigators in different cities and at different times, the interrogated rightists all confirmed the same facts. Bukharin's closest friends and students voluntarily told the entire truth."[235]

Concluded Ezhov, anti-climactically: "It seems to me that Bukharin and Rykov fully answer for the activities of rightist organizations and for their anti-Soviet activities. This raises the question as to whether they can remain on the Central Committee or in the party."[236]

Anastas Mikoian then rose to speak. He began by praising Stalin "for according Bukharin and Rykov the opportunity to gather the facts with an abundance of caution to determine whether the charges against them are true"—despite their use of "tears and prayers to play on the sympathies of delegates." Mikoian defended the NKVD, which he called the legitimate "weapon of the party," against Bukharin's charge "that the investigators are making up testimony." To doubt that the investigation was thorough and fair would be a "rotten attack on our Central Committee."

Mikoian sought to demonstrate that Bukharin was a "master of lies" by refuting his statement to the December plenum that he had not seen [accuser] Kulikov since 1929. In his confrontation with Kulikov two days later, Bukharin remembered meeting him in 1932 on a street corner. According to Kulikov, Bukharin had given him assassination orders at this meeting, something which he could scarcely forget. Mikoian drove home that this was only one of the many examples of Bukharin "lying without shame."

Bukharin could only weakly retort to each charge: "You lie" or "I'll explain it all."[237]

Mikoian depicted Bukharin as a subhuman, who infiltrated the party "with monsters, not people but animals who appear to support the party line but in fact do the opposite."[238] Mikoian reiterated Ezhov's complete confidence in Bukharin's guilt, which was "clear to a blind man."[239] Bukharin's refusal to admit his obvious guilt was an "anti-party" act. Loyal party members would voluntarily confess and ask forgiveness.

Like Ezhov before him, Mikoian appeared to leave the fate of Bukharin and Rykov to the delegates: "Now, Comrades, there arises the question, after all that has been proven without doubt, what kind of candidate members are these? What kind of party members are these?" [Voice: "What kind of citizens?"]

Bukharin faced a heckling and hostile audience as he began his defense. Interrupted repeatedly, he had to plead with the audience: "Don't scream at me. I'll answer everything."[240] His remarks, according to the transcript, were met with derisive laughter. Bukharin acted as his own defense attorney (or "devil's advocate," as the crowd shouted out). Somehow, he had to demonstrate that the multiple charges against him were all lies, misunderstandings, hearsay, or memory lapses.

He began with the admission that his own testimony suffered "from small, private memory lapses," pointing out that even Molotov had forgotten that he presided over a speech Bukharin had given at the Bolshoi Theater.[241] He could not possibly remember every meeting he'd had over the past eight years. He had barely seen Rykov and Tomskii since their defeat, although they were supposed to be leaders of these plots. And although he had cut off contacts with friends and students, they have been "put to shame by their association with me both in gossip and in print." (Ezhov countered: "But you wrote personal letters to your friends in 1934 and 1935, whom *you* are putting to shame.")[242]

Bukharin stated that he should not be held responsible for inflammatory statements of those who were part of his school. Under such a standard, "I would be responsible for Tomskii's death because, if I had not headed the rightists in 1928 and 1929, maybe his fate would have been different."[243]

The assertion of his right to defend himself elicited a bitter exchange with Mikoian:

> **BUKHARIN:** Mikoian says that I am trying to discredit the testimony against me. But, Comrade Mikoian, how could it be otherwise? If I want to discredit something, I myself must discredit it. If I am not allowed to challenge the evidence, my defense becomes useless.

MIKOIAN: I said that you have the right to criticize but in a Bolshevik—not in an anti-party—fashion.[244]

Undeterred, Bukharin began to point out the many inconsistencies in the evidence, such as a witness telling one story in interrogation and a completely different story at his trial, and "no one takes notice, as if this is the way things should be!"[245] or inconsistent statements on which official (Stalin or Kaganovich) Bukharin ordered him to assassinate.[246] It became clear that the facts were not important to the impatient crowd. When Bukharin pointed out: "I was not in Moscow at the time (of the purported conspiratorial meeting). I was in Northern Kirgizia," a voice called out, "Well, you prepared the meeting and then left." Bukharin shot back, "They testified that I met a number of people at this meeting. . . . In this case, the lying is completely clear."[247]

Bukharin's litany of inconsistencies elicited an outburst from the indignant Kaganovich: "But dozens of witnesses have said these things!"

BUKHARIN: No, you said you were terribly impressed with the testimony of Kulikov and characterized it as fully consistent. I demonstrated that Kulikov's testimony was far from consistent.

KAGANOVICH: No.

BUKHARIN: How come "no"? What I say is absolutely true.[248]

As Bukharin continued to challenge the testimony of his accusers, Stalin finally intervened. He methodically recited a list of Bukharin's accusers—all former friends and colleagues (including Valentin Astrov and Aleksandr Slepkov)—asking about each one, "Why should Astrov lie?[249] Why should Slepkov lie? This only added to his problems."

Bukharin's weak response: "I don't know. . . . You have to understand the psychology of people.

STALIN: No. No. No. Excuse me, but can we establish the facts? At the confrontations, where we were all present, the Politburo was there, Astrov was there along with other defendants. When I or someone else asked each of them, "Say truthfully, are you giving this testimony freely or are you being forced? Radek even broke into tears when asked this question—how could it be forced? It was voluntary. Astrov made a good impression. . . . We all felt sorry for him. Astrov is an honest man who does not know how to lie. He was disturbed. He turned to you several times: "You organized us. You made us enemies of the party and you now want to avoid responsibility. You should be ashamed."

Bukharin responded in frustration: "I am not able to convince you otherwise if you think they told the truth that I gave terrorist orders, but this is an unbelievable lie which I cannot take seriously.

STALIN: Maybe you were just gossiping and then forgot.
BUKHARIN: I never said such a thing.
STALIN: You talk a lot.
BUKHARIN: I agree that I talk a lot, but not about terror. This is absolute nonsense.

Stalin had indeed come to the heart of the matter. If Bukharin was innocent, why were so many of his colleagues, friends, and students testifying against him? Bukharin probably knew the real answer. They had been coerced by the NKVD, but he could not say that in the open plenum. It was well known that the NKVD was run directly by Stalin. To accuse the NKVD was the same as accusing Stalin.

The next day, the plenum was turned over to delegates eager to demonstrate their rage at the "animals" who wished to destroy the party and their beloved Stalin. "Orators" lined up to speak, while others contributed to the circus-like atmosphere by hurling insults from the audience. Not that the insults safeguarded those who hurled them: of the thirteen delegates who spoke against Bukharin that day, seven would be executed during the Great Terror.[250]

The speakers demanded harsh punishment. Among the comments: "Bukharin knows perfectly well how such crimes are punished. People are shot for these crimes. . . . Not reporting knowledge of terrorist acts is the same as participation in terrorist acts. . . . The place for such criminals is on the judgment bench."

Bukharin's sympathizers in the crowd had to remain silent. After the plenum, Bukharin told Larina that Lenin's sister, Mariia Ul'ianova, wiped away tears with her handkerchief as she watched her friend's

anguish.[251] Each of the more than two hundred spectators understood that one false word or even expression could put them in
Bukharin's shoes.

It was a party tradition to make verbatim transcripts of Central
Committee plenums. Each speaker, even those under attack, was allowed to edit his remarks. Later, in prison, Bukharin went to great
lengths to edit and polish his testimony. Most of those who spoke
against him rewrote their remarks to make them even more stri-
dent. One may wonder why an "enemy of the state" like Bukharin
was accorded such a privilege? The answer is that Stalin determined
what would and what would not be printed. Stalin played yet another trick on Bukharin: the published transcripts of the February–
March plenum omitted entirely the material "On the Case of Comrades Bukharin and Rykov." Bukharin's defense thus disappeared
into the deep vaults of the Central Committee archives, not to be
revisited for over a half century.

CHAPTER 34

February 27, 1937:
For or Against the Death Penalty?

T
HE PLENUM DEBATE ended uncharacteristically, without Stalin giving instruction on what to do with the defendants. Instead, the Bukharin-Rykov case was turned over to a thirty-six-person commission for a recommendation on punishment. In addition to Stalin himself, the commission's membership included Politburo members (Molotov, Mikoian, and Voroshilov), major-city party bosses (Moscow's Khrushchev and Leningrad's Andrei Zhdanov), regional party heads, and two known Bukharin supporters—Lenin's sister, Mariia Ul'ianova, and his widow, Nadezhda Krupskaya. Stalin added the two women for window dressing; they dared not be lenient toward Bukharin.

Stalin wanted it to be known that it was the party that was condemning Bukharin, not he.

The commission members must have been in a quandary. If they proposed leniency, Stalin might question their own devotion to the cause. Having seen what was happening to Bukharin and Rykov, they had to be very careful. In fact, seven of the twenty members whose recommendations were recorded were eventually executed.

The committee met on February 27. The transcript of its proceedings lists recommendations of twenty commission members, although there were thirty-five members.[252] The major disagreement was over the death penalty. The recommendations appear to have been made in the following order (eventual purge victims are shown in bold type):

1. **Ezhov:** Turn them over to the military tribunal with a recommendation for the highest measure of punishment—shooting.
2. **Postyshev** (Ukrainian party boss, then under threat of investigation): Turn them over to the court without shooting them.
3. Budennyi: Turn them over to the courts and shoot them.
4. Stalin: Do not turn them over to the courts. Direct the case of Bukarin-Rykov to the NKVD.
5. Manuil'skii: Turn them over to the courts and shoot them.
6. Shkiriatov: Turn them over to the courts but do not shoot them.
7. **Antipov:** The same.
8. Khrushchev: The same.
9. Nikolaev: The same.
10. Ul'ianova: For Stalin's proposal.
11. Shvrenik: Turn them over to the court and shoot them.
12. **Kosior:** Turn them over to the court and do not shoot them.
13. Petrovskii: Turn them over to the court and do not shoot them.
14. Litvinov: The same.
15. Krupskaya: For Comrade Stalin's proposal.
16. **Kosarev:** Turn over to court and shoot them.
17. **Iakir:** The same.
18. **Vareikis:** For Comrade Stalin's proposal.
19. **Molotov:** For Comrade Stalin's proposal.
20. Voroshilov: For Comrade Stalin's proposal.

Thus, eight commission members voted against the death penalty. Six voted for it, and six voted for Stalin's proposal to turn the matter over to the NKVD.

A second ballot followed. All the commissioners now knew what Stalin wanted, and true to form, they swung unanimously to Stalin's position. They made their recommendation to "turn Bukharin and Rykov's case over to the NKVD." The Central Committee adopted a resolution to this effect on March 3.

We can only speculate about the true dynamics of this meeting. Stalin's proposal was fourth. One would have expected subsequent commissioners to fall in behind him, but only five of the remaining sixteen voted for his proposal. Four voted for execution, perhaps to show radical devotion, but seven voted *against* it. One certainly wonders why? It is possible that Stalin at this time did not have the support of the party leadership to execute Bukharin and Rykov.

In any case, the mix of proposals fit Stalin's plans. He realized that this was not the time to execute Bukharin. He was still claiming his innocence, so execution would send him to his grave without his confession. Further, the commission members could not know that Stalin was planning a third (and final) Moscow Show Trial featuring Bukharin. Stalin's proposal was the equivalent of a death sentence anyway. It meant that the NKVD was to prepare Bukharin for his public trial. The bullet to the back of his head could wait.

CHAPTER 35

February 27, 1937:
Arrest Warrant for "Bukharin, N. I."

T HE FOLLOWING DOCUMENT circulated for approval in the NKVD's Lubyanka headquarters on the very day the commission handed in its recommendation:[253]

Warrant AK-3

The investigation of the Trotsky-Anti-Soviet Center established that, along with the counter-revolutionary terrorist activity of the Trotsky organization, there existed a parallel counter-revolutionary underground organization of rightists carrying out the same activity. It also established that the counter-revolutionary organization of rightists has its own center, one participant of which is Bukharin, N. I. The investigation and court case of the anti-Soviet Trotsky center, in particular, the testimony of Piatakov, Radek and Sokol'nikov, established that the Trotsky organization entered into contact with the counter-revolutionary organization of the rightists.

The sentenced Piatakov and Radek revealed that they were connected with members of the center of the organization of rightists by Bukharin, N. I. In conjunction with the ongoing investigation, it was established that Bukharin, N. I. played a leading role in this organization.

The head of the First Department of the State Security Administration and the deputy head of the NKVD signed the warrant. So did the state prosecutor, Andrey Vyshinsky, who scrawled, "I approve."

Of the three signers of Bukharin's arrest warrant, only one—Vyshinsky—would survive. The security administration chief committed suicide five months later, probably in anticipation of arrest, and the NKVD deputy head was executed in August 1938, as Stalin's Great Terror underwent its final spasms.

CHAPTER 36

February 27, 1937:
Arrest and Parting

NIKOLAI BUKHARIN'S TESTIMONY and cross-examination ended on February 25. It was left to him and the family to wait for the other shoe to drop. Two days later, it did, as Stalin wasted no time after receiving the commission's verdict. A phone call from his secretary summoned Bukharin to the plenum; the secretary told him to hurry over there, complaining that he was holding up the session.

But Bukharin did not hurry. He was determined to linger awhile with his extended family in their shared Kremlin apartment. He began by saying good-bye to his ailing father and first wife Nadezhda. Then he fell to his knees before Anna Larina to beg forgiveness for her ruined life, and urged her to raise their infant son as a "Bolshevik without fail." He asked her to fight for his vindication and to remember every word of his testament. "You are young and will live," he declared.

As Bukharin put on his leather jacket and opened the door, Anna Larina bade him farewell with the words: "See that you do not lie about yourself."

When Bukharin arrived at Sverdlov Hall, he was surrounded by NKVD officers and taken to the Lubyanka prison.

Shortly thereafter, a dozen or so NKVD officers, headed by the notorious chief of the investigations department, Boris Berman, arrived to conduct a thorough search of the apartment. Berman was incongruously dressed as if going to a banquet: stylish black suit and white shirt, a dazzling ring on his finger. His first question to

Larina was "Any weapons?" She opened a drawer and extracted a revolver given to her husband by the defense minister, Voroshilov. It bore the inscription, now bitterly ironic, "To the leader of the Great Proletarian Revolution."

Bukharin's soon-to-be-confiscated "archive" of letters, papers, and photographs was strewn on the floor in disarray. It was crudely bundled together and shipped off in a truck. At midnight, the NKVD officers prepared themselves a feast from the Bukharin's meager food supplies. When Anna refused their invitation to join them, the NKVD officer in charge quipped: "Could it be that you have decided to follow Bukharin's example and announce a hunger strike?" Her answer: "I won't eat at the same table with you or sit on the same floor."

After their meal (which probably included healthy shots of vodka), the intruders began to sing. Larina went to tell them to quiet down because they were waking the baby. They said they were about to depart anyway, but left behind women investigators with orders to turn the pages of all the books in Bukharin's library.[254]

CHAPTER 37

February 1937:
Anna Larina Is Betrayed

THE TIME WAS EARLY FEBRUARY 1937, shortly before Bukharin's arrest. He and Larina had been essentially secluded in their Kremlin apartment since August. She received a telephone call from her former classmate and fellow Komsomol organizer, Kolya Sozykin, who was visiting Moscow and staying in a nearby hotel. He invited her to drop by. Bukharin warned her that the invitation sounded like a trap: Sozykin was from Stalingrad and worked there, so why was he suddenly in Moscow at a hotel reserved for the party elite?

Although she wanted to stay close to her husband, the isolated Larina needed, as he himself recognized, "a breath of fresh air." He told her to go ahead and visit Sozykin, but warned as she left, "Just don't say anything unnecessary."[255]

Hungering to talk with an old friend she felt she could trust, Larina told Sozykin everything: the confrontations, the plenums; Bukharin's absolute denial of wrong-doing. She restrained herself only by avoiding mention of Stalin's name. When Sozykin asked what Stalin's role was, Larina replied circumspectly that the NKVD was deceiving him.

As she returned from the rendezvous, she encountered Ordzhonikidze coming out of his Kremlin apartment. Despite his long friendship with Stalin, Comrade Sergo was also feeling the Master's wrath. His closest associates had been arrested, and his brother was under investigation. He gazed at Anna with eyes full of grief, squeezed her hand, and told her to "stand firm." Before long, he too would be dead.

After her husband's arrest, Larina saw Kolya Sozykin one more time at his hotel. She poured out to him the story of Bukharin's brutal treatment at the February plenum and his ensuing arrest. Sozykin tried to calm her, assuring her that things would be sorted out. He offered candy and toys for the baby.

Shortly thereafter, Larina was called to the Lubyanka to bring books that her husband had requested. As she was about to leave, Sozykin called and offered to accompany her. He arrived with oranges for her to pass on to her husband. In gratitude, Larina kept her meetings with her old friend secret throughout all her subsequent interrogations—only to learn, almost two years later, that he was indeed a plant. Her informant was none other than the new NKVD head, Beriia, who told her that Sozykin "gave a very bad report on you" after their meetings.

Sozykin's betrayal was a bitter pill for Anna, but an important cautionary tale. When she entered the Gulag system, she was warned that virtually everyone around her would be an informer. Indeed, throughout her imprisonment, she was constantly informed on by seemingly sympathetic fellow prisoners.

CHAPTER 38

April 1937:
Impossible Dream

Bukharin slept fitfully in his small cell in the NKVD's Internal Prison in the bowels of the Lubyanka, light years away from his Kremlin apartment. His nocturnal writing was interrupted by fitful sleep, often marked by hallucinations. In them, Bukharin saw Stalin and Nadezhda, Stalin's wife who committed suicide. In one, Nadezhda came to him and asked, "What are they doing with you? I'll tell Iosif [Stalin] that he should come to fetch you." He knew that Nadezhda would never believe that he would do something bad against her Iosif.

The dream was so real that Bukharin wanted to immediately write to Stalin to come to take him from this place. As the dream continued, he found himself talking with the Master for more than an hour, hoping to make an impression with his devotion.

Awakening to the harsh reality of his prison cell, Bukharin remembered an exchange almost a decade earlier in which Stalin said to him, "You know why I treasure you? You are not capable of intriguing?" He also remembered his immediate answer: "Yes, but at that very time, I ran to Kamenev." He wanted to tell Stalin: "Whether you believe it or not, this fact stands out in my mind as the original sin stands out for the Jews. My god, was I a child and a fool."[256]

CHAPTER 39

June 2, 1937:
Bukharin's Cagey Confession

NIKOLAI BUKHARIN was arrested on February 27, 1937, and he was turned over to the NKVD to extract a credible confession. Bukharin had vehemently denied all the charges against him and was determined to fight for his "political honor." He already knew that the defendants in the first two Moscow Show Trials (Kamenev, Zinovyev, Piatakov, and others) were "no longer among the living"—even though they had dutifully confessed to all charges. Bukharin also knew that he could not believe any promises about the safety of Anna and the rest of his family. His NKVD interrogators, therefore, appeared to have little leverage over him.

In prison, Bukharin kept himself occupied with what he did best—writing—while his interrogators worked on him to confess. He turned his attention to articles, essays, and a semi-autobiographical novel. These "prison writings" would be preserved and published after the fall of Communism.[257] Bukharin's day was spent with interrogations, confrontations, and negotiations both with NKVD officers and with the state prosecutor, Vyshinsky. At night, he wrote.

The stakes associated with a confession from Bukharin were high. The success of the Master's planned third Moscow Show Trial hinged on a public confession from Bukharin in an open forum before an international audience. A confession of political opposition or general knowledge of the terrorist intentions of others would not be enough. Bukharin had to admit to plotting murder, espionage, and violent overthrow of the government.

The fact that a growing number of former party leaders— Zinovyev, Kamenev, and the military high command—had been or were shortly to be executed for such crimes meant that Bukharin had to admit to them as well. After all, they were all supposed to have been in the plot together.

On June 2, slightly more than three months after his arrest, Bukharin signed a handwritten "Personal Confession of N. Bukharin." It numbered fifteen typewritten pages, each page initialed and, in some cases, edited by Bukharin himself.[258] "This confession," he wrote, "gives a general picture of the counter-revolutionary activity of the rightists and their allies."

To what did he confess? Bukharin admitted that, after political defeat in 1929, he and his allies chose a policy of "capitulation," publicly agreeing to toe the party line while taking their resistance underground using "tactics of deception." Stalin had unwittingly spread a cadre of purged rightists throughout the country, ready to recruit new sympathizers beyond the vigilant eye of Moscow.

Bukharin explained that the success of collectivization and dekulakization stabilized Stalin's hold on power. Therefore, he and his allies had to overthrow Stalin by force. For this, they adopted a new (Riutin) platform, which called for the overthrow of Stalin via a palace coup. The platform was also shown to Zinovyev and Kamenev, and both accepted it. (Bukharin, who had forcefully denied even reading the platform in February, maintained in his confession that he was little involved in its drafting.)

Bukharin's confession proceeded to explain that their ragtag band of conspirators recruited powerful but unlikely allies to carry out the planned palace coup and assassinations. They included Genrikh Iagoda (the head of the NKVD), Avel' Enukidze (Stalin's confidant in charge of Kremlin security), and Marshall Mikhail Tukhachevskii, along with other generals. There was also a German connection. Their co-conspirator, Trotsky, had already agreed with the Nazis to partition the USSR after a German attack, and they maintained contacts with German spies posing as businessmen.

The "rightist-leftist" conspiratorial bloc, according to the confession, assigned Enukidze to carry out the palace coup under the direction of Tomskii. Unfortunately, Stalin got wind of their plot and executed Enukidze. Iagoda, who was in charge of the investigation, however, made sure that the rightists were not implicated—until, that is, he himself was unmasked.

Bukharin named forty-two co-conspirators (not including émigrés living abroad). Most had already been arrested. The best they could hope for now would be a long prison term. Most would be executed.

Bukharin's confession was far from perfect for Stalin's purposes. It provided precious little detail that would have proven his guilt. Bukharin confessed only to being part of a vague plan to overthrow Stalin, but the alleged conspirators seem not to have met, had no operational plans, and included individuals most unlikely to betray Stalin. Bukharin, unlike Kamenev and Zinovyev, refused to admit to actual killings. Throughout, he subtly downplayed his role. If he was really a leader of the conspiracy, he was a remarkably detached one.

No one knows for sure why Bukharin confessed and under what circumstances. Interrogators surely offered assurances for family members, but if anything, the treatment of Bukharin's extended family became worse after his confession.[259] The most likely explanation is that he was tortured. Evidence from a 1988 hearing on his case suggests that Bukharin was tortured by a feared interrogator (one L. R. Sheinin of the Saratov NKVD), starting the first of June.[260] Bukharin apparently succumbed quickly and signed his confession the next day. (Sheinin was arrested in 1950 and served a short term in prison.)[261]

Stalin could not have been fully confident that Bukharin's confession would stand up in an open show trial with foreign observers and press present. To put him on the stand would be a risk. Foreigners might wonder how such a master plan could be put into action based on chance meetings and street-corner conversations. Clearly Stalin needed a fully compliant and cooperative Bukharin at the trial. For once, therefore, Bukharin had an advantage over Stalin. He knew that death sentences were carried out almost immediately. There would not be time for torture. If he saved his "betrayal of the party" to the end, he would "no longer be among the living" within a mercifully short time.

CHAPTER 40

June 1937:
Anna Meets a New Widow

AFTER NIKOLAI'S ARREST, Anna Larina was allowed to stay in their Kremlin apartment for some three months. Thereafter, she moved to the elite House on the Embankment, where she lived with her baby, Bukharin's father, and Nadezhda Lukina. Nadezhda kept her stash of poison ready for when the NKVD came for her. (When its agents finally did, she took the poison but was revived so that she could be executed later.) Bukharin's elderly father, a former math teacher, sat at a table solving algebra problems, muttering, "My Kol'ka a traitor? What nonsense!"

Bukharin left behind no savings. He donated his wages and royalties to the party fund, and only accepted payments from the Academy of Sciences. He had ignored his family's needs in favor of a political apparatus that would execute him. When a bill came for the rent, Larina wrote the authorities, saying that the fascist intelligence services "did not provide financially for their hireling," so she was returning the bill unpaid. Thereafter, no further bill came.

In June 1937, the doorbell rang. Nadezhda grabbed for her poison just to be sure as an NKVD officer entered carrying a leather bag. He put Larina's passport in his bag and handed her an order signed by Ezhov. It gave her a choice of exile in one of five cities. The officer politely recommended Astrakhan as the proper place, noting that "It has the Volga, and there are fresh fruits and melons."

Larina refused to sign the order or to leave voluntarily, saying, "You can evict me from here only by force." She did sign a receipt acknowledging that she had been apprised of the order. Two days later, at ten p.m., Anna was taken to the Lubyanka by Ezhov's deputy, who explained that she could avoid exile by denouncing Bukharin in the press. She refused, and her request to see him was denied. A few days later, an NKVD officer came to the House on the Embankment with a car and a truck to transport her to the train station and her belongings to Astrakhan.

In preparation for exile, Larina had left Iura with her mother, Lena, who was suffering from tuberculosis. (Lena herself was arrested six months later.) Bukharin's father then took twenty-month-old Iura to live with him. But the old man died shortly thereafter, and the boy was placed in the first of a number of orphanages, his father an enduring mystery to him.

As an exile, Larina was allowed to ride on the train to Astrakhan without an escort. Watching the expansive steppes unfold, she glanced at her neighbor's newspaper announcing the execution of the "traitorous" high military command. The news saddened her because she had admired Marshalls Tukhachevskii, Iakir, and Uborevich.

In the compartment, the other passengers began a heated discussion of that shocking development: "They couldn't have been tried for nothing . . . Just look at what harm they did . . . They themselves confessed; they did!" Only one passenger, dressed in a Ukrainian blouse, defended the officers: "I knew Iakir and fought under him in the civil war, so I know what kind of a man he is. A fascist hireling? That's absurd, a filthy lie. He's Jewish, you know, so like hell he needs fascists."

As this argument continued, Larina noticed three women nearby—one older, another in her thirties, and a young girl. They looked familiar, and she exchanged places with the passenger sitting next to them. Anna said directly to the younger woman: "I am the wife of Nikolai Ivanovich," avoiding her husband's last name because he was known by his name and patronymic.

The answer came back immediately: "And I, of Mikhail Nikolaevich." Larina thus became acquainted with Marshall Mikhail Tukhachevksii's new widow, and his mother and daughter.[262] Anna would join the ranks of new widows some nine months later.

In Astrakhan, Larina met other wives and families of "traitors of the people," and began a routine of looking for quarters and work. Shortly after she found a job at a fish cannery, officials presented her with a search warrant and arrest order on September 21, 1937. Larina succeeded in concealing a photo of Bukharin in her shoe. She was taken to the Astrakhan prison, where her interrogations began. She refused to admit that her husband was a spy and that she had been assigned to recruit him. In December, Larina was sentenced to eight years in prison and consigned to the Tomsk camp for wives of traitors.

Thus began Anna's odyssey through the Gulag, which would not end until 1945.

CHAPTER 41

March 2–13, 1938:
Twenty-one on Trial

FOR THE TRIAL OF BUKHARIN and twenty co-defendants, Stalin chose the stately Union House. It was originally built in 1780 by a princely family, then, in 1919, turned over to the trade unions, becoming a venue for congresses and conventions. Lenin's body had lain in state there. Earlier, its Hall of Columns hosted symphonic concerts conducted by Tchaikovsky and Rimsky-Korsakov; Rachmaninov and Chaliapin performed there as well.

Because the building was located near the Kremlin, on Bolshaya Dmitrovka Street, Bukharin and Larina passed by it regularly. In fact, it was in front of the Union House that they decided to marry.

When the sensational trial opened—with Andrey Vyshinsky prosecuting and Col. General V. V. Ul'rikh presiding as chief judge—such festive occasions lay deep in the past. The hall was jammed with officials, foreign diplomats, and journalists. Admission was by ticket only, and the audience was stacked with NKVD officers posing as ordinary citizens.

As Vyshinsky delivered the indictments, the audience jumped to its feet demanding death for the vile enemies of the people. Other "popular" denunciations of the twenty-one followed. Throughout the eleven-day trial, crowds gathered outside the Union House and throughout Moscow to call for the ultimate penalty.

The defendants included Bukharin and Rykov, diplomat and former justice official Nikolai Krestinskii, former NKVD head Genrikh Iagoda, former ministers of the government, leaders of Central

Asian republics (who supposedly plotted against the Soviet Union with Lawrence of Arabia), and three doctors who had signed death certificates (probably falsifying the cause of death) of prominent party leaders and writers.

Vyshinsky's opening statement of March 11 whipped the crowd into a frenzy. He accused the defendants of committing "the vilest, most abominable crimes," and described them as the "bestial faces of international brigands," "slaves of intelligence services," "a pack of hangmen and underground assassins," "the lowest creatures ever known in the history of mankind."[263] Vyshinsky's incendiary language was designed to repulse and incite and to destroy any sympathetic sentiments. The defendants' crimes were horrific and included murders—and plots to murder—"by means of special drugs."

Vyshinsky ended his tirade as follows: "The entire country demands one thing: shoot the plotters as foul dogs, crush the accursed vipers. The years will pass and the graves of traitors will be overgrown with wild weeds and thistles, while bright rays of our sun will shine over the fatherland."

Each defendant was called to the stand to undergo examination by Vyshinsky, who summarized the evidence against them and listed their crimes. He cited at length from the testimony of their accusers. Although the defendants were assigned token defense attorneys, they had to answer the charges themselves. Most did not dispute the charges or testimony against them. No witnesses were called. Most were in prison or dead.

Bukharin was an exception. Throughout his testimony, he stubbornly fought with Vyshinsky over the facts of the case. Bukharin vehemently denied participating in murder and foreign espionage. Although these exchanges drove Vyshinsky to near hysteria, Bukharin appeared to be sparring about details, not about the fundamentals of his confession—that he had been part of a massive conspiracy to overthrow Stalin and his regime.

When Larina heard the trial reports, she first thought that Bukharin might have been replaced by a stand-in. She became convinced that the man in the dock was actually her husband when she later learned that one of his best friends, writer Il'ia Erenburg, had been forced to attend the trial on Stalin's instructions to "let him see his friend." Erenburg was sickened by what he saw: "It all appeared to me as an unbearable nightmare, and I could not even tell straight out my wife and daughter."[264] Other attendees reported strange speech patterns and gestures from defendants, as if they were signaling to each other what was really going on.

Each of the defendants duly confessed their guilt, with one hitch: Nikolai Krestinskii decided at the last minute to plead not guilty. A break was hastily called because "all were tired." Krestinskii was taken away to be worked over. When the court re-adjourned, Krestinskii stated: "In the face of world public opinion, I had not the strength to admit the truth that I had been conducting a Trotskyite struggle all along. I request the Court to register my statement that I fully and completely admit that I am guilty of all the gravest charges brought against me personally, and that I admit my complete responsibility for the treason and treachery I have committed."[265]

Krestinskii's act of resistance remained in the trial record. On reading Krestinskii's words, Anna Larina wrote, "tears shot from my eyes. It seemed to me that I could actually see Krestinskii's kindly face with his myopic eyes peering through thick glasses."[266]

Before the judges' verdict was delivered, each defendant was given an opportunity to make a final statement to the court. In all cases, except Bukharin, they reaffirmed their guilt and expressed profound regret for their actions. (Bukharin's remarkable final statement appears in the next chapter.) On March 13, the court sentenced all but two defendants to death. They received twenty-five years in prison.

According to Soviet criminal practice, the sentences were to be carried out quickly. Each defendant, however, was allowed to appeal for mercy to the Supreme Soviet of the USSR. Most of the defendants wrote a short paragraph, knowing that the exercise would be useless. But Bukharin, true to form, composed a lengthy missive asking for a pardon "on his bended knees" and promising that, if pardoned, he would work tirelessly for the good of Soviet society.[267] To no one's surprise, each appeal was denied, and preparations began for the executions.

Stalin's goal in orchestrating this third Moscow Show Trial was to convince Russia and the world that the Soviet regime was surrounded by domestic and foreign enemies. If they were not dealt with decisively and mercilessly, all could be lost. A public trial was a risky strategy, but it worked.

Most foreign observers concluded that the charges and confessions were genuine. The *New York Times*, the *Nation*, and the *New Republic* treated the trial as a legitimate judicial proceeding. Despite the fact that the *Times* bureau chief was arrested in the middle of the trial on trumped-up charges, he concluded that the trial was not a fake and that the use of torture did not necessarily mean the confessions were untrue.[268]

Although the tone-deaf foreign press was struck by the fierce exchanges between Bukharin and Vyshinksy, its members concluded that the two were sparring over details. The *Times* correspondent's report mentioned only that Krestinskii's change of heart "impressed foreign hearers as strange."[269]

Not only the press was taken in: the U. S. Ambassador, Joseph Davies, wrote in a dispatch to Washington that "the Kremlin's fears were well justified. For it now seems that a plot existed, in early November 1936, to project a coup d'etat, with Tukhachevskii as its head, for May of the following year. Apparently it was touch and go at that time whether it would actually be staged."[270]

The German embassy, in contrast, understood exactly what was going on. Embassy analysts knew the charge that the defendants worked as German agents was false, and they concluded that the trial was conducted to allow Stalin to rid himself of political enemies. Their concern, however, was to minimize damage to Germany from the trial, not to expose it as a farce.[271]

The world paid close attention to Bukharin's trial. It was heatedly debated in liberal and socialist circles in Europe and the United States. European socialists liked and admired Bukharin, whom they knew from his work in the Comintern. He therefore had his defenders. British and American socialists, however, maintained that the trial was fair, even that it "represented a new triumph in the history of progress."[272] An open letter to American liberals was circulated for signatures in support of the trial.[273]

How did Stalin get away with staging Bukharin's show trial? There are a number of likely explanations. First, few outside of Russia could imagine the extreme torture and intimidation that Stalin was prepared to use. The spectacle of former ministers, generals, and industry leaders standing in the dock and confessing to incredible crimes overwhelmed outside observers. Second, in socialist and social democratic circles, Stalin's Russia was viewed as mankind's best effort. Judging the trial a sham would mean that Soviet Russia was run by ruthless thugs and criminals and was scarcely the beacon of hope they considered it to be.

Third, although history had produced its share of tyrants, few got a good look at Stalin's rule. He had closed his country off from the rest of the world. Few could even imagine the depths of his despotism. His image was that of a kindly, smiling "Uncle Joe" (the nickname assigned him by the American press during World War II). How could a man like that be credibly accused of such evil deeds?

CHAPTER 42

March 12, 1938:
Papering over Bukharin's Final Defiance

I N HIS FINAL LETTER TO STALIN, on December 10, 1937, Bukharin had told him that although innocent of the charges, he would not retract his confession at his trial. In general terms, he kept to this promise until his final statement.

The courtroom was hushed as Bukharin began to read from his prepared text of his final statement on the evening of March 12, one day before his death sentence was to be pronounced. Unlike the other defendants, whose last statements dutifully and tamely confirmed their guilt and pled for mercy, Bukharin used his remarks to undermine the foundation of his confession.

To the shock of Vyshinsky and Ul'rikh, he embedded his final statement with exaggerated language and double entendres. According to some witnesses, he used bizarre gestures to signal his utter disregard for the proceeding and especially for "citizen general prosecutor" Vyshinsky. Employing sarcasm and nuance, Bukharin denied virtually all the substantive charges against him and proceeded to show their lack of logic, indeed, their lunacy. He then thrust a sword through the heart of the trial: the "Rightist-Trotsky Bloc," he declared, did not even exist, its members never met, and charges of espionage were ridiculous!

At long last, Stalin appeared to have been outwitted by Bukharin.

The resourceful Stalin could not let Bukharin's most damaging statements gain wide circulation. (He was extremely lucky that Bukharin's remarks were not picked up by the foreign press, which was also present.) Stalin immediately ordered the films of the trial buried deep in Politburo vaults—where they still languish.

Stalin could not let Bukharin's betrayal alter his plan to publish a full transcript of the entire trial. Stalin proceeded to publish the transcripts with his own twists; although he could not leave out Bukharin's final plea in its entirety, he could redact Bukharin's most telling denials and evident sarcasm. Stalin was a master editor and up to the job.

Indeed, the trial transcript was published shortly after the trial. Many thought this was the true transcript, until the sensational publication in 1996 of the text of Bukharin's final statement—read in open court as edited for publication by Stalin in heavy pencil.[274] We now know what Bukharin actually said and what Stalin removed from the printed version.

The transcript allows us to reconstruct the frenzied courtroom scene on the evening of March 12, 1937, as Bukharin dutifully began his last words by "declaring myself politically responsible for the totality of crimes committed by the Rightist-Trotskyite bloc." Thereafter, Bukharin careened widely off the script that he was expected to follow.

Stalin had to mark out his next statement: "I accept responsibility even for those crimes about which I did not know or about which I did not have the slightest idea." He then redacted Bukharin's most sarcastic and devastating blow to the prosecution: "I deny most of all the prosecutor's charge that I belonged to the group sitting on the court bench with me, because such a group never existed!" If there had been no such thing as a "Rightist-Trotsky bloc," how could it be the subject of criminal prosecution?

Although Stalin the censor allowed some of Bukharin's subsequent sarcasm to pass (for example, "members of a bandit group must at least know each other"), he struck out the sarcastic remark that it made no sense for foreign intelligence to create "non-existent groups."

Stalin also edited out Bukharin's dismissal of charges of espionage ("It is necessary to describe me as a fool to attribute all these things to me. . . . We would have gained nothing but empty promises"). In addition, he could not accept Bukharin's demolition of evidence that he had worked for the Japanese based on reports in Tokyo newspapers: "And how is it that the Japanese identify their agents publicly? A strange position."

Bukharin closed his discussion of espionage charges with extreme sarcasm that Stalin probably hoped would be interpreted literally: "I, however, declare myself guilty of the evil plan to break apart the USSR, because Trotsky agreed on territorial concessions, and I was with Trotsky in a [non-existent] bloc. This I admit."

By now, it was clear that Bukharin was making a travesty of the proceedings, and the court officials moved to shut him up. Stalin had to redact the presiding judge's warning and Bukharin's defiant response:

> CHAIRMAN: Accused Bukharin—You speak about yourself and what you are experiencing, others speak about themselves, about their rebirth, etc. But what you are talking about is not the last word of an accused.
> BUKHARIN: Excuse me. I thought I can talk about anything in my last words.
> CHAIRMAN: You are diverging too far from your last word. Don't forget that this *is* your last word.
> BUKHARIN: I asked you, citizen chairman of the court, if I can talk about anything, and you answered affirmatively.
> CHAIRMAN: This does not mean you can go to the absurd.

Stalin allowed Bukharin's final words to stand despite their hyperbole:

> Comrade Chairman, it is possible that I am speaking the last time in my life, and I ask you to let me finish my speech. I explain why I came to the necessity to capitulate. We acted against the joy of the new life using the most criminal methods of struggle. I deny the accusation that I tried to assassinate Lenin, but my counter-revolutionary co-conspirators, with me at their head, tried to kill the work of Lenin, continued by Stalin with gigantic successes. The logic of this struggle, step by step, sunk us into a black swamp.... But now the counterrevolutionary banditry has been destroyed, we are beaten, and we have repented our terrible crimes.

The official transcript of 1938, even with Stalin's edits, already raised serious doubts about the trial, brought on by Krestinskii's denial of guilt and the uncensored parts of Bukharin's final statement.[275]

The most authoritative demonstration of the sham nature of the proceedings had to wait until Stephen Cohen's 1971 biography of Bukharin. Cohen, using the official transcript and other evidence, was able to demonstrate how Bukharin "tore the case against him to bits" in what "may fairly be called his finest hour."[276]

CHAPTER 43

March 15, 1938:
The Ultimate Payback: A Ghastly Death

ANNA LARINA HOPED that her husband had died honorably, declaring his innocence. Fortunately, she did not know the gruesome circumstances of his execution. And we do not know whether Stalin would have imposed them if Bukharin had "behaved" better at his trial. We can be confident that Stalin had personally orchestrated Bukharin's execution as he had his trial. The Master met regularly with Ezhov to plan the interrogations, and during breaks in the trial, he received reports from prosecutor Vyshinsky.[277] Rumor had it that he sat concealed behind a curtain in the courtroom. Some said that they could even see puffs of smoke from his pipe.

As the trial date approached, Bukharin understood that execution was likely. In his final, early-December letter to Stalin from his cell, Bukharin made a last plea to the only person who could grant his request:

Very Secret-Personal
To: Stalin, Iosif Vissarionovich
If I'm to receive the death sentence, then I implore you beforehand, I entreat you, by all that you hold dear, not to have me shot. Let me drink poison in my cell instead. For me, this point is extremely important. I don't know what words I should summon up in order to entreat you to grant me this as an act of mercy. Politically, it won't really matter, and, besides, no one will know a thing about it. Have pity on me! Surely you'll understand, knowing me as well as you do.[278]

Stalin brushed aside the plea in a final sadistic act. According to one account of the execution: "NKVD officer Litvin told me in 1938 in Leningrad that he was present at the execution of Bukharin and sixteen other co-defendants. From his account, I remember that Frinovskii [deputy head of the NKVD] ordered that Rykov [a known alcoholic] be given a bottle of whiskey, which he drank before his execution. But Bukharin suffered one last, cruel—and macabre—prank. He was given a chair so that he could watch as the others were shot."[279] And Stalin saved his execution till the last, deliberately heightening, sixteen times over, the anguish of the condemned man who had pleaded not to be killed with a bullet to the back of his head.

The head of the Lefortovo Prison, Captain of State Security Petr Maggo, carried out the shootings. He was awarded the Order of the Red Star for his service in the battle against counter-revolutionaries. Arrested a year later, Maggo disappeared.[280]

CHAPTER 44

May 1938:
Anna's Own Ordeal

IN MAY 1938, Anna Larina was transferred to Novosibirsk, the location of the investigations department of the Siblag camp. She was surprised to learn the identity of the driver waiting to take her to the prison: he was the chauffer of the purged West Siberian party head who had hosted her and Nikolai shortly after their marriage. At that time, the animal-loving Bukharin had with him an owl he was taking back to Moscow.

The driver now asked her: "Did you get the owl back to Moscow safely?" Larina managed a quip: "We got the owl there, all right. But when we did, they arrested it."

Her cell was in an underground chamber. As she entered it, rats scurried away. The guard gave her a pail to scoop out the water that covered the floor. She awoke next morning covered with fleabites and itching all over. She had to remove her clothes to shake out the fleas.

Larina's interrogator was a man of about forty-five. She heard that he had been reduced in rank and was now exceptionally ferocious to fend off a further demotion. He began his questioning by saying that he knew she had belonged to a counter-revolutionary youth organization and had been assigned as a liaison with Bukharin. If she did not name her fellow conspirators, she would rot in prison.

She denied the accusation, saying that Bukharin was a revolutionary, not a counter-revolutionary; therefore, she could not be a liaison with counter-revolutionaries. Her response set off a tirade: "Insolent bitch! Counter-revolutionary swine! Even after the trial, you dare state that Bukharin was not a counter-revolutionary?" He continued: "Will you say you had no relationship with Bukharin at all?"

ANNA: No, I will not say that. I was his wife.

INTERROGATOR: His wife? We know for a fact that your marriage was a fiction to cover Bukharin's counter-revolutionary ties with young people.

(The stunned Anna pointed out that they had a child together.)

INTERROGATOR: It has yet to be proved, yet to be demonstrated, by whom you had this child.

(The session turned into a shouting match.)

INTERROGATOR: There is no place for you on Soviet soil. Shoot her! Shoot her!

ANNA: It is you who should sit behind bars, not me. Shoot me right now! I don't want to live.

Finally, the interrogator fell silent. He picked up the phone and indifferently ordered the guard to take her back to her cell. As she fell into a troubled sleep, a rat jumped onto her leg. That triggered fright and revulsion, but as time passed, the rat brightened her solitude; the guards were surprised that she fed it bread.[281]

CHAPTER 45

December 1938:
Back from the Precipice

L ARINA AND OTHER WIVES of convicted traitors were shuttled from one prison to another. In early December 1938, she found herself in the Antibes camp, not far from the Siberian town of Mariinsk, which housed a regional investigations division.

In the course of her odyssey, Larina had been threatened with execution if she did not confess. In the Antibes camp, her interrogator had once led her in the direction of the ravine where executions took place, but turned back when she did not fall for his bluff. She knew that executions required a signed execution order, and none had been issued.

Later that month, what she described as her "moment of glory" arrived. She was led to Antibes' investigation section, where an official from the nearby Mariinsk camp presented her with an official document, stating that "Counter-revolutionary scum must be swept form the face of the earth." Everything went dark before her eyes when she made out the words "supreme penalty."

Larina had prepared herself psychologically for such a moment. She did not fear death itself but the moment before it. Numbness seized her as two men with revolvers in holsters led her down the road past her cell and in the direction of the ravine used for executions. In the hazy distance, she could see the dreadful place.

But as the group approached the very edge of the ravine, a man in a light-colored fur jacket ran toward them, shouting that the prisoner should be taken back. So once again she was led away from the deadly ravine. Passing by her cell, she saw that the jailor had carried out her suitcase. She had been recalled to Moscow for interrogation.[282]

CHAPTER 46

Late December 1938: Advice from a Mass Murderer

IN DECEMBER 1938, Larina found herself in the NKVD's Internal Prison, where her husband had spent his last days. Told she was to meet the NKVD commissar himself, she dressed in her remaining presentable clothes. As she passed through the bustling corridors, guards snapped their fingers—a pre-arranged signal to close office doors so that people being interrogated did not see one another.

Expecting to meet her husband's executioner, Nikolai Ezhov, Larina was shocked to be greeted by Lavrentii Beriia, who had twice hosted her in Georgia. She even remembered Beriia's toast in 1928: "Let's drink to the health of this little girl. May she live long and be happy." Approaching his desk now, she burst out: "Where has our glorious people's commissar Ezhov gone, the one who terrified the wasp's nest of enemies of the people?"[283]

She got no answer. But the ever-charming Beriia assumed the role of gracious host, calling for food, praising Larina's beauty, and asking what kind of work she was doing in the camp (response: cleaning toilets). He then opened her thick file and extracted a letter she had written to Ezhov from prison requesting that he have her shot.

As she later recalled the meeting, Beriia asked her, "Do you really not want to live? This is hard to believe. You are so young; you have your whole life ahead of you." When she hesitated in responding, he added, "It is not possible to execute someone repeatedly. Execution is one time only. And Ezhov surely would have shot you"—if Stalin had wanted her killed.

She answered now with a question: "Well, are you going to execute me?" Said Beriia, "That all depends on how you conduct yourself."

He then got down to business. There was an ongoing investigation of the foreign minister, Maksim Litvinov. Beriia wanted to know if Larina knew of (or was willing to fabricate) any relationship between Litvinov and Bukharin. The two men, she replied, were not close at all; Litvinov never visited her husband.

Beriia tried again to persuade her to implicate Litvinov. "Did you know Valentin Astrov?" he asked. "He helped us a lot, and we spared his life." She knew that Astrov had been one of Bukharin's protégés. Now Beriia pointed out that because he had testified against Bukharin, he was freed and given an apartment in Moscow.[284] (In later life, Astrov would admit that he was persuaded to lie in "a political document to show my full break with counter-revolutionary-rightist opportunism.")[285]

When Larina still refused, Beriia shouted at her, "Forget your conscience! You blab too much! If you want to live, then shut up about Bukharin. If you don't shut up, here is what you'll get."[286] He aimed his forefinger at his temple. After that dramatic gesture, she promised herself to remain silent on that score; she sensed that for some reason Beriia wanted to save her life.

Returning to her cell, she wrote a letter to Stalin: "Through the thick walls of this prison, I am looking at you straight in the eyes. I do not believe in this monstrous judicial process. What you had to gain by putting Nikolai Ivanovich to death, I cannot understand."[287]

The letter had to go through Beriia. He never delivered it.

CHAPTER 47

Summer of 1956:
Reunion with Iura

AFTER HER MEETING WITH BERIIA in December 1938, Anna Larina again disappeared into the camps of Western Siberia. Stalin had ended the Great Terror a month earlier; his attention turned to the growing threat of war with Germany. A new generation of younger party leaders took the places of those executed. Bukharin's name disappeared from history books, as did his photographs. It was as if he had never existed.

The Siberian camps that incarcerated Larina began to empty of able-bodied men after the German invasion of June 1941. They were sent to the front to sweep for mines or do other tasks that carried with them almost certain death. Those who remained in the camps were faced with reduced rations and soaring mortality. The camps themselves, except for those with the most dangerous prisoners, were increasingly short of guards.

In many camps, inmates lived outside the walls of the prison. They fraternized openly, even married. But when their prison terms expired, few were allowed to leave the immediate region. They continued to live near their old camps, serving as prison administrators and even guards.

Larina met and married her second husband, Fedor Fadeiev, in a prison camp. The couple had two children. Fadeiev followed her to her various places of exile after her release from prison in 1945. Anna was no longer in prison, but she was told where to live. Although the name of her famous first husband had faded from public view, Russia's new rulers would not allow the widow of Nikolai Bukharin to return to her Moscow.

The year 1956 found Anna Larina and family in a Western Siberian village not far from the Antibe camp, where she was nearly executed eighteen years earlier. Although many Gulag prisoners had been released following Stalin's death in 1953, it was not until 1956—the year in which Nikita Khrushchev denounced Stalin—that political prisoners began to be released in large numbers. Communications with the world outside the Gulag had become easier, and Larina's attempts to locate her son, Iura, bore fruit.

Through relatives and other contacts, she obtained the address of the now twenty-year-old Iura. She managed to get a letter to him.[288] She got one in return from him:

> Dear Mama: I received your letter and I have thought a great deal about many things and have many questions. I don't understand everything in my life. Why did I leave my family's home and where is my father? I would be very grateful if you'd answer these questions.[289]

It was arranged for Iura to travel to his mother's village in Siberia.

Larina, Fadeiev, and their two children, then ten and six, were living forty-five kilometers from the nearest train station. They set out in a motorcycle with a sidecar, survived a road accident that almost killed them, and arrived on time at the train station. Larina had not seen Iura since the beginning of her odyssey through the Gulag in June 1937. Now a young man, he was using the name Iura Gusman, the surname of the last relatives with whom he had lived before entering orphanages and foster homes.

On the road to the station, she wondered what kind of man Iura had become after such a disconnected childhood. Would he reproach her for the trials he had endured? Should she reveal the full story of his father?

As her son's train arrived, Larina anxiously searched the faces of the descending passengers. She had only her son's baby picture with which to identify him.

Suddenly she felt an embrace and a kiss. Although he had not seen her photograph since he was a child, Iura had picked *her* out of the crowd. His simple explanation: "I noticed a woman pacing on the platform. I realized right away it was Mama. She was very skinny. Both of us were very skinny."[290]

Searching her son's face for familiar features, Larina found none that were conclusive. But when he spoke, his voice was that of his father.

Back in their village, Larina put off for several days Iura's questioning about his father. She finally volunteered that he "had been one of the top ten party leaders." Noting his mother's continued reticence, Iura suggested that he try to guess who his father was— "and if I guess right, you will tell me." After some thought, Iura announced: "My father was Bukharin, Nikolai Ivanovich." After twenty years of wondering who his parents were, Iura finally knew.

Soon after he left the settlement, Iura wrote to his mother. He needed her and his father's dates of birth to fill out for his school graduation papers. He now took the name he was given at birth, Iura Nikolaevich Bukharin. Although he had trained as an engineer, he shared his father's love of art and became a professional artist. He and his older half sister, Svetlana Gurvich, would go on to assist his mother in her quest to fulfill their father's wish for reinstatement in the Communist party.

CHAPTER 48

February 5, 1988: Rehabilitated by Old Men

O N FEBRUARY 5, 1988, the Soviet Supreme Court announced Nikolai Bukharin's full exoneration from criminal charges.[291] The Politburo's concurrent recognition of that decision fulfilled Bukharin's last, desperate dream—fifty years after he gave his testament to Anna Larina—of rehabilitation by a "future generation" of party leaders.

The leaders who restored his "honor" were cautious bureaucrats in their seventies, and they themselves would lose their positions within a few years as the Communist party collapsed. They were acting only because their boss, Mikhail Gorbachev, had ordered them to do so.

The road to rehabilitation began with Larina's return to Moscow in 1959, the year her second husband died. She lived quietly there while privately petitioning each Soviet leader, from Khrushchev to Gorbachev, to take up Bukharin's cause. With expectations raised by the "thaw" that Khrushchev had set in motion, she submitted a text of Bukharin's testament to the Central Committee. Khrushchev's fall in September 1964 dashed hopes for quick action, but she persevered.[292] Her son Iura and stepdaughter, Svetlana, aided in the campaign.[293]

A powerful literary tool also came into play: the clandestine translation of Stephen Cohen's noted biography of Bukharin.[294] Cohen's work introduced Bukharin's ideas concerning an alternative form of socialism for Russia, chronicled his power struggle with Stalin, and informed readers of his innocence of the charges for which he was executed. The book received a wide readership in Russian underground intellectual circles. Many young Russians for the first time learned the name and story of an important national figure who had been excised from their history books.

In 1977, in response to an appeal by the Bukharin family, the Italian communist party and the Bertrand Russell Peace Foundation circulated a petition calling for Bukharin's rehabilitation. Cohen arranged for an English-language version of Larina's memoirs. The publication of the memoirs and the growing renown of Cohen's biography led to a "Bukharin boom," just as Gorbachev was embarking on his program of reform in 1987.

Under his prompting, the state prosecutor formally protested Bukharin's March 1938 conviction to the Soviet Supreme Court. As the court initiated its review of the legal charges, Gorbachev formed a Politburo commission to review the "political" side of the case. This commission, composed of Politburo and Central Committee members, and supported by faceless technical experts (probably from the KGB), met on January 5, 1988.

The commission members, uncomfortable with Gorbachev's new policy of glasnost', did not appear to welcome their task. They decided they could minimize the release of information (276 volumes of case materials) by simply recognizing the Supreme Court decision to rehabilitate Bukharin and adding a line or two of their own—something that could be done in little time and with little effort. The commission worried about press and public attention; if word got out, its members might be swamped by inquiries and demands for records.

Another procedural question was whether to reconsider the convictions of all twenty-one defendants tried in 1938 or only Bukharin and Rykov. Commission members agreed that at least one member of the "bloc" (NKVD head Iagoda) could not be rehabilitated because he had himself committed criminal acts as head of the NKVD ("If people ask about Iagoda, we can say it is a separate case").

With these procedural issues out of the way, the commission began its review of the Bukharin case. The KGB had provided boxes of documents and sent its archival expert to answer questions. Regrettably, his report was not recorded, but the commissioners' questions were. Their first question was: "When you examined the Bukharin case, he declared himself guilty on all points except espionage and murder. Do you have materials on how his guilty plea was obtained and why he denied certain charges and accepted others?"

The expert's answer: "We have materials that show forbidden methods usually used to obtain confessions." (That response confirms that Bukharin was tortured but does not explain exactly what the "forbidden methods" were.) The expert added, "We have testimony that some were offered their lives. We have the names of those who say this."

The commission then discussed the specific charges against Bukharin: "It is important that we clearly understand of what he was accused . . . what was said in the accusatory conclusions by his interrogators, how they carried out the investigation, and how Bukharin answered. . . . We need to see what accusations remained after his denials." Frustrating their examination was the fact that Bukharin's confession was edited by Stalin, and he himself was given no chance to sign off on it. (No wonder: he was executed shortly after the trial.)

The commissioners exhibited their curiosity about court procedures, as they asked: "Did the court try to obtain evidence about the testimony of his accusers?" Answer: "There are only the confessions of the accused themselves." Question: "Do we have the testimony of the accusers, and did they testify before the court?" Answer: "The court did not call them. The witnesses did not participate. There were no defense attorneys."

The members found themselves puzzled by Bukharin's so-called crimes. One member said, "Some of us have read the sentence. Many of the offenses ascribed to him, are these really crimes?" Another commissioner recognized that Bukharin's so-called confession was actually a defense: "If we look at the substance, he denied everything." Another commissioner concluded: "With respect to the criminal case, he did not confess, and there is no proof offered."

Bukharin's statement that the "Rightist-Trotsky bloc," charged with committing the crimes, did not exist prompted the following exchange:

FIRST COMMISSIONER:[295] What does our commission think about whether the "Rightist-Trotskyite" bloc existed or not? It appears that the Supreme Court review will not address this issue.

SECOND COMMISSIONER:[296] Should we say that we rehabilitate him only with respect to criminal charges or should we address political issues? No matter what we decide, we will never understand the nuances of that time. The commission should limit its report to the kind of opposition there was; was it a worker, leftist, or rightist opposition?

THIRD COMMISSIONER:[297] But is this the truth?

SECOND COMMISSIONER: In my opinion, we must decide only about criminal matters. Questions of politics are questions for the history of our party.

FOURTH COMMISSIONER:[298] If we don't deal with this [political] issue, we will not decide the case.

SECOND COMMISSIONER: From a legal point of view, we must associate a bloc with some sort of organization. Such an organization did not exist.

At least a majority of the commission agreed, in effect concurring with Bukharin that the "Rightist-Trotskyite bloc" did not exist "as an organization." But the commission's discomfort with the question of "blocs" and "opposition" remained. Rehabilitating Bukharin could encourage anyone punished for opposing the party line to apply for rehabilitation. As one commissioner put it, "Today it is Bukharin, but tomorrow it could be Zinovyev and Kamenev, persons directly connected with Trotsky, who did occupy an anti-Soviet, anti-state position."

In the end, the commission recommended a minimalist approach in the form of a decree issued on February 5, 1988:

"To accept as a matter of record the decree of the plenum of the USSR Supreme Court about the reversal of the sentence of the Military Collegium of the Supreme Court of the USSR from March 13, 1938 with respect to N. I. Bukharin, A. I. Rykov, and others and the cessation of the case due to the absence of criminal acts."

Thus, Bukharin's "future generation of party leaders" rehabilitated him with a whimper. There were no trumpets or triumphal ringing of bells—as in the finale of Tchaikovsky's 1812 Overture. They did not condemn the court procedures used to convict Bukharin or his execution on political grounds.

The ultimate irony is that Anna Larina's battle for her husband's rehabilitation had to wait until the party was on its last legs. Both she and Bukharin believed firmly in socialism, believed that the Stalin years were a transitory time of troubles, and that a new generation of enlightened party leaders would emerge. But the party leaders whom Mikhail Gorbachev ordered to reinstate Bukharin were dull bureaucrats, uninterested in true justice and resentful of being given such a distasteful task. What could have been an ending on a high note turned into another disappointment.

Within three years, the party membership card of the reinstated Nikolai Bukharin disappeared into the vaults of a defunct organization. To add insult to the gravest of injuries, public opinion in contemporary Russia continues to rate Joseph Stalin among the top figures in the nation's history. Nowhere in such polls is the name Nikolai Bukharin mentioned. In death, Stalin has again outwitted—and outdistanced—Bukharin.

CHAPTER 49

A Special (Specially Tardy) Delivery

NIKOLAI BUKHARIN'S farewell letter to Anna Larina reached her in June 1992. In her memoirs, she writes only that she received it "unofficially." Possibly it was sent to her by a sympathetic archivist who did not want to be identified. More than a half-century had passed since he wrote it to her from prison. Why the record-setting delay? The answer is simple: under Stalin, the writer's declaration of innocence alone made the letter undeliverable.

Denied a last visit with her husband, and despite the ridiculous tardiness of the letter, we can imagine her joy and sorrow as she read it. Written a mere three months before he admitted his guilt on a world stage, the wording is guarded; Bukharin knew, of course, that this intimate communication would be read by a number of people, probably including Stalin himself. Reproduced in part below, the letter, in addition to asserting innocence, expresses undying love and devotion.

To: Anna Mikhailovna Larina
    Dear Sweet Annushka, My Darling!
    I write to you on the eve of my trial . . . with a special purpose, which I emphasize three times over: no matter what you read, no matter what you hear, no matter how horrible these things may be, no matter what might be said about me or what I might say—endure everything courageously and calmly. Prepare the family. Help all of them. I fear for you and the others, but most about you.
    Don't feel malice about anything. Remember that the great cause of the USSR lives on, and this is the most important thing. Personal fates are transitory and wretched by comparison. A great ordeal awaits you.

I beg you, my dearest, muster all your strength, tighten all the strings of your heart, but don't allow them to break. . . .

It is not appropriate for me to say more about my feelings right now. But you can read between the lines how much and how deeply I love you. Help me by fulfilling my request during what will be for me a difficult time. Regardless of what happens and no matter what the outcome of the trial, I will see you afterwards, and I will be able to kiss your hands.

Good-bye my darling, Your Kol'ka

January 15, 1938[299]

Anna Larina died on February 24, 1996, four years after receiving the farewell letter. Her Moscow funeral was attended by her family, friends, and admirers who knew Nikolai Bukharin and his ideas through her memoir of their life together and what she called his "afterlife."

Along with other Stalin victims, Nikolai Bukharin was buried in a common grave on the grounds of the Kommunarka estate, on which NKVD dachas stood. Occasional ceremonies there commemorate him and other party leaders killed by Stalin.

CHAPTER 50

Bukharin, Stalin, and the Bolshevik Revolution

STALIN'S KILLING OF MILLIONS, most of them ordinary people rather than party politicos, perversely explains why Russians remain split on whether he was a hero or a monster. They somehow weigh the fact of having killed those millions against such other statistics as growth, modernization, and victory in war. Each and every victim had his or her story. We cannot examine all of their tragedies; we can only tell the stories of a few, but they personalize the tragedy embodied in the gruesome statistics of Stalin's killing fields.[300]

If Nikolai Bukharin and Anna Larina had been just an ordinary couple caught in Stalin's madhouse, their story would still be worth telling. Bukharin said to her in his farewell letter, "Personal fates are transitory and wretched"; yet these two intersected the course of history. This book has sought to shed light on how the world's first socialist state went terribly wrong and why it was likely to veer off course.

We study history in retrospect; we already know how things turned out. Stalin won. Bukharin lost, along with many others. He was executed after a sham court trial. Trotsky fell to Stalin's assassin. Many other Bolshevik founding fathers went to the execution grounds without ceremony or subsequent reconsideration. And it was Stalin's vision, not Bukharin's, that in the end molded the USSR.

Some consider Stalin's victory predestined. Others marvel at how unlikely it was. If I could have somehow transported myself back to January 27, 1924, as somber party leaders carried Lenin's coffin out of the Union House, I would at that point have come down on the "unlikely" side. Now, however, after closely studying Stalin's conduct of the power struggle, I conclude that his success was the *most likely* outcome.

The significance of Nikolai Bukharin depends on whether he could have prevailed over Stalin. On this key issue, the literature is divided. Stephen Cohen argues that Bukharin, as the "favorite of the party," indeed stood a good chance to succeed Lenin.[301] Bukharin's fatal error was that he did not go public with his disagreements with Stalin until it was too late. Miklós Kun, in his later biography of Bukharin, also maintains that he had a real chance to create a united front against Stalin. He had potent allies who controlled the machinery of state, the trade unions, and, early on, the Moscow party organization. Even though Bukharin did not have administrative skills, he could have rallied those who did; and he had a large number of loyal supporters in the party base.[302]

At the opposite end of the spectrum, the distinguished British historian E. H. Carr argued that Bukharin was a relatively insignificant figure. He never occupied a party position of real authority; he never really stood a chance against the better-organized Stalin; he did not have firm views. It is only Bukharin's appeal as a personality, coupled with his tragic fate, that kept him in the public eye.[303]

F. A. Hayek, in his 1944 *Road to Serfdom*, used economic logic to conclude that the victory of a Stalin-like figure was inevitable. Hayek argued that in what he termed "administered economies," the most brutal and cruel figure among the potential leaders inevitably wins power struggles.[304] Stalin may have had rivals in the brutality category (Trotsky, Zinovyev, Kaganovich), but they lacked his planning and organizational abilities. And they were somewhat restrained by moral principles. Of the potential successors to Lenin, Stalin had the comparative advantage in cruelty that Hayek considered decisive. By this measure, if not others as well, Bukharin trailed badly.

The power struggle of the late 1920s gains particular significance in that it took place at a real turning point of Russian history. Unlike hypothetical "counterfactual analysis," the Bolsheviks had to make a real choice. Were they to build on a mixed economy underpinned by peasant agriculture? Or were they to follow Stalin's course of forced industrialization and collectivization?[305]

Bukharin would be rediscovered and rehabilitated under Mikhail Gorbachev.[306] By then, however, the Soviet Union had become a nation of huge state enterprises manned by indifferent workers and state farms populated by elderly people—too late to follow the course laid out by Bukharin.

The protagonists could not have been more different. Nikolai Bukharin was gregarious, full of joy, intellectually curious, sensitive, and fascinated by the world around him. His parents were schoolteachers, who raised him in a loving home. He loved to write on philosophy, politics, literature, poetry, and the arts. He tended to think the best of others. He was widely liked within the party. Despite three marriages, his family life was happy; he remained on good terms with his ex-wives.

Both in his youth and as an adult, Bukharin frequently became ill when he suffered setbacks, leading him to retreat from political fights. Many considered him too "soft" and emotional, perhaps even a crybaby. He had no talent for political infighting and intrigue. He talked and wrote too much, and became characterized by detractors as a windbag. He was easily outwitted by Stalin. The man who became the Master thought things through beforehand, while Bukharin acted impulsively and emotionally.

Stalin was born to a poor, dysfunctional family. He was ashamed of his mother, and his alcoholic father abandoned him. There were rumors that he was the product of one of his mother's many affairs. He grew up in street gangs in Georgia, where violence, revenge, and retribution were facts of daily life. Although he received a truncated seminary education, he spent his youth in radical and revolutionary pursuits that called for terror, murder, and violence. Stalin worked hard to compensate for his deficient formal education. He read prodigiously, maintaining a massive personal library and annotating as well as absorbing its contents. Whereas Lenin was an armchair terrorist, who pardoned victims when their relatives appealed to him,

Stalin was the real thing, a man who relished revenge and the killing of enemies.

As a grown man, his family life continued the earlier patterns. He neglected his aging mother. He quarreled with his sons (neither of whom amounted to anything) and abused his second wife, who committed suicide. He had no real friends. Fellow party leaders who did not offer unquestioning loyalty had to be—and were—removed. Jealousy often drove Stalin. He never forgot insults or slights. But he was a man of great patience, willing to wait to exact revenge for years or decades.

Bukharin was not a saint. He was content to use Stalin's control of the party machinery to defeat his own ideological enemies, but he protested indignantly when Stalin turned the same weapon on him. As he saw himself losing to Stalin, he began to grovel and tried effusive flattery. He deserted colleagues and friends alike to demonstrate his obeisance to the Master. When innocents were condemned, Bukharin pretended that he, too, believed in their guilt. His confession was full of names of friends and colleagues—a virtual death sentence for them.

Stalin conducted the power struggle according to Hayek's formulation. His opponents miscalculated the depth of his lust for power as well as his lack of conscience or loyalty. As he once remarked, "Loyalty is a malady that affects dogs." Unlike others who were bound by friendships or associations, he sacrificed friends and relatives, such as his daugher's godfather and his own brother-in-law, without hesitation.

Among the contenders, only Stalin appeared to have a concrete plan. Trotsky expected to be anointed leader; Bukharin hoped to rally influential allies and followers through his brilliance. His was a battle of ideas against brute force.

By controlling the Central Committee, Stalin became the equivalent of the party; he decided disputes, set agendas, and appointed supporters to key positions. Any disagreement with him became a betrayal of the party. His opponents lost because they were not disagreeing with Stalin but with "the party." Stalin could set rules and also set them aside. When Bukharin demanded his right to party arbitration in his conflicts with Stalin, the Central Committee, aka Stalin, simply ruled against him.

Bukharin and Stalin had markedly different visions of socialism. Until these differences in visions became apparent, Bukharin saw no need to battle with Stalin. It was not by chance that their first skirmishes were over the use of force in the countryside, an area where they clashed over fundamental policy.

Bukharin's vision was what today might be called "socialism with a human face." There would be a monopoly Communist party, but its one-party rule would be less intrusive and threatening than Stalin's. Peasants would be allowed to live their own lives, sell to whom they wanted, and join collective farms only if they wished. Bukharin's socialism would have established economic incentives and focused on arrangements that promoted efficiency. Heavy industry would have been state owned but most likely cautioned to operate with an eye to markets and even profit.

In clear contrast to Stalin, Bukharin once declared, in a debate with political adversaries, "I know I am not the party." He was content to be one of many, sharing in collective rule. After it became obvious that Stalin was aiming for one-man domination, Bukharin sought to gather around him influential party members who, like him, lacked Stalin's power to intimidate and bully but held common policy views.

For Bukharin, success would have been a stable system of collective rule that made the types of policy decisions he favored. His job: to construct the system's ideology. The actual governing would be left to others.

We cannot know whether Bukharin's vision would have succeeded. It was never tried. Too often, Bukharin's admirers assume his program would have worked, but it would have required a delicate balancing act. It is hard to imagine, however, that the program could have turned out worse than what actually happened.

To conclude that Stalin was the most likely winner does not rule out other outcomes. Stalin's victory could have been thwarted by any number of chance factors. Lenin could have regained enough of his health to engineer Stalin's removal. A random assassin could have killed Stalin at any time—as an anarchist bomb almost did Bukharin in 1918. Trotsky could have been a better politician and less of an egoist. Other Politburo members could have followed Lenin's advice to remove Stalin. None of these events happened, but they could have—dumping Stalin's best-laid plans on the ash heap of history.

Was Bukharin guilty or innocent? With few exceptions, historians argue—and Gorbachev's commission agreed—that he was innocent of the charges on which he was executed. That view is correct if we judge his guilt by participation in actual murders, assassination plots, or espionage. Indictments relating to those charges were pure fiction.

But whether Bukharin was guilty of a capital offense under Stalin's standards is another question entirely. In an absolute dictatorship, the dictator defines what constitutes a crime.[307] In Stalin's mind, loose talk of "removal," idle threats issued in a drunken stupor, or simply wishful thinking that the Master would die deserved the death penalty. Stalin's closest associates, Lazar Kaganovich and V. M. Molotov, both of whom lived to see the Gorbachev era, agreed; so he was not alone.[308] Stalin's minister of oil, Nikolai Baibakov, who lived until 2008, argued that the Bukharin-like ideas of Gorbachev killed the Soviet Union.[309]

Judged by Stalin's standards, Bukharin was guilty. During the dekulakization campaign, he would surely have been rooting for Stalin's failure—and would have shared these thoughts with his closest colleagues. Like-minded friends and colleagues would have engaged in outbursts against Stalin. Kamenev's notes of their July 1928 meeting, which Bukharin never really denied, reveal the depths of hatred of Stalin. Also, when Bukharin's friends and colleagues were interrogated, much of what they said about the tone of their conversations rings true.

Judged by less-authoritarian judicial standards, the case against Bukharin strikes a false note. Grandiose plots were hatched in furtive meetings and certainly resembled idle gossip. That a hotheaded ally volunteered to kill Stalin at a drunken party does not make for a serious plot.[310] No one could cite a single joint meeting attended by any two of the various factions that constituted the "mad dogs" reviled at Bukharin's trial. Western jurisprudence would have required real acts, but for Stalin, gossip and chatter were more than enough.

This brings us to a final point: why did Bukharin confess? His execution lay only three years in the past when the Hungarian-born British novelist, Arthur Koestler, published *Darkness at Noon*—a fictionalized account of Bukharin's interrogation that is now considered a literary classic.[311] According to Koestler's theory, Bukharin confessed voluntarily after he was convinced that his death was a necessary part of the revolutionary dialectic. Although such an interpretation is consistent with Bukharin's romantic character and makes for good fiction, it has little factual support.

Not until Stephen Cohen's 1971 biography was there an account based on the then-incomplete historical record.[312] Cohen demonstrated that Bukharin resisted confessing for four months despite the pressure of constant interrogations. More important, the author showed that in his trial, Bukharin retracted his already watered-down confession.

In this account, I have introduced new evidence showing that Bukharin was tortured. We now have much of the archival record on Bukharin's interrogation and trial. This material contradicts Koestler's fictionalized account that the confession was voluntary.

In his last days in prison, with his trial approaching, Nikolai Bukharin realized that he would not have the time to complete his autobiographical novel. With reluctance, he wrote "The End" after the fourth chapter.

And as his trial and execution loomed, all Bukharin could see was his insignificance. He found comfort only in the fact that his suffering would soon be over. He concluded with this eloquent and poignant observation:

> There is an end for everything on this earth; there is also an end to the torture of passing uncertainty, when you swallow the last concealed tear of your soul, and the crisis transforms itself into some new phase, which is destined to disappear in the eternal passage of time.[313]

∞

Notes

1. Although this quotation is commonly attributed to Stalin, it cannot be found in his writings.

2. Simon Sebag Montefiore, *The Young Stalin* (New York: Alfred A. Knopf, 2007), 68–89.

3. Paul Gregory and Norman Naimark, eds., *The Lost Politburo Transcripts: From Collective Rule to Stalin's Dictatorship* (New Haven: Yale University Press, 2008), 16–17.

4. N. V. Petrov, ed., "Karatel'naia sistema: struktura i kadry" in V. P. Kozlov, *Istoriia Stalinskogo Gulaga* (Moscow: Rosspen, 2004), vol. II, *Decree of the Cheka*, "About Red Terror," September 2, 1918, 523.

5. Paul Gregory, *Terror by Quota: State Security from Lenin to Stalin* (New Haven: Yale University Press, 2009), 119–121.

6. Paul Gregory, *Lenin's Brain and Other Tales from the Secret Soviet Archives* (Stanford, CA: Hoover Press, 2008), 80–89.

7. Miklós Kun, *Bukharin: Ego druz'ia i vragi* (Moscow: Respublika, 1992), 84–85.

8. Paul Gregory, "The Politburo's Role as Revealed by the Lost Transcripts," in Gregory and Naimark, *Politburo Transcripts,* 16–17.

9. These figures are cited from *History of the Communist Party of the Soviet Union (Bolsheviks)*, edited by Commission of the Central Committee of the CPSU (Bolsheviks) (Moscow: International Publishers Co., 1939), 232, 296, 320.

10. Boris Bazhanov (translated by David Doyle), *Bazhanov and the Damnation of Stalin* (Columbus: Ohio State University Press, 1990), 106.

11. Gregory, *Lenin's Brain,* 113.

12. www.izvestia.ru/obshestvo/article3125409/ (accessed November 21, 2009).

13. Bazhanov, *Damnation of Stalin,* 100–102.

14. www.historyguide.org/Europe/testament.html (accessed November 19, 2009).

15. Stephen Cohen, *Bukharin and the Bolshevik Revolution: A Political Biography, 1888–1938* (New York: Alfred A. Knopf, 1973), 288–290.

16. O. V. Khlevniuk et al., *Stalin i Kaganovich Perepiski: 1931–1936 gg.* (Moscow: Rosspen, 2001), 558.

17. Bazhanov, *Damnation of Stalin,* 40.

18. Anna Larina, *This I Cannot Forget: The Memoirs of Nikolai Bukharin's Widow* (New York: W.W. Norton, 1988), 118.

19. Letter from Stalin to Ordzhonikidze, dated September 24, 1930. Cited in Oleg Khlevniuk, *Politburo: Mekhanizmy politicheskoi vlasti v 30-e gody* (Moscow: Rosspen, 1998), 37.

20. Cohen, *Bukharin*, 289.

21. Larina, *This I Cannot Forget*, 64.

22. Cohen, *Bukharin*, 369.

23. Bazhanov, *Damnation of Stalin*, 44–45.

24. Letter of N. I. Bukharin to I. V. Stalin from the Internal Prison of the NKVD, *Istochnik*, 2000. No. 3, 56–58.

25. V. P. Danilov, O. V. Khlevniuk, A. Iu. Vatlin, et al., eds., *Kak lomali NEP, Stenogrammy plenumov TsK VKP(b) 1928–1929 gg.*, 5 vols., vol. 1, *Ob"edinennyi plenum TsK i TsKK VKP(b) 6-11 aprelia 1928g.*; vol. 2, *Plenum TsK VKP(b) 4-12 iiulia 1928g.*; vol. 3, *Plenum TsK VKP(b) 16-24 noiabria 1928g.*; vol. 4, *Ob"edinennyi plenum TsK i TsKK VKP(b) 16-23 aprelia 1929g.*; vol. 5, *Plenum TsK VKP(b) 10-17 noiabria 1929g.* (Moskva: Mezhdunarodnyi fond "Demokratiia," 2000), 4:644.

26. Larina, *This I Cannot Forget*, 213.

27. This material is purported to be from Bukharin's OGPU file as of August 1929; cited by V. M. Zhukhrai, *Stalin: Pravda i lozh'* (Moscow: Svarog, 1996). Also see Kun, *Bukharin: Ego druz'ia i vragi*, 64–65.

28. Aleksandr Vatlin and Larisa Malashenko, *Piggy Foxy and the Sword of Revolution* (New Haven: Yale University Press, 2006).

29. Larina, *This I Cannot Forget*, 127.

30. Statement of Klement Voroshilov. Cited in J. Arch Getty and Oleg Naumov, *The Road to Terror: Stalin and the Destruction of the Bolsheviks, 1932–1939* (New Haven: Yale University Press, 1999), 102.

31. Bazhanov, *The Damnation of Stalin*, 15.

32. E. H. Carr, "The Legend of Bukharin," *Times Literary Supplement*, September 20, 1974, 1.

33. Carr, "The Legend of Bukharin," 1.

34. Kun, *Bukharin*, 102.

35. Carr, "The Legend of Bukharin," 1.

36. Larina, *This I Cannot Forget*, 140.

37. "No ia-to znaiu, chto ia prav," *Istochnik*, 2003, 49 (letter of Bukharin to Stalin, April 15, 1937).

38. James Young, "Bolshevik Wives: A Study of Soviet Elite Society," PhD diss., Sydney University, 2008.

39. Larina, *This I Cannot Forget*, 65.

40. Larina, *This I Cannot Forget*, 74.

41. Larina, *This I Cannot Forget*, 115.

42. Larina, *This I Cannot Forget*, 110.

43. Larina, *This I Cannot Forget*, 229.

44. Quoted in Cohen, *Bukharin*, 240.

45. The transcript of this meeting is found in Aleksandr Vatlin, Oleg Khlevniuk, and Paul Gregory, eds., *Stenogrammy zasedanii Politbiuro TsK RKP(b), 1923–1938* (Moscow: Rosspen, 2009), vol. 1, 579–580, 595.

46. Larina, *This I Cannot Forget*, 221–223.

47. Svetlana Allilueva, *Dvadtsat' pisem k drugu* (New York: Harper Collins, 1967), 29.

48. N. I. Bukharin, *Izbrannye proizvedeniia* (Moscow: Izdatel'stvo politicheskoi literatury, 1988), 195–197.

49. Paul Gregory, "The Agricultural Surplus Hypothesis: A Retrospective," *Europe-Asia Studies*, Vol. 61, No. 4, 2009, 669–683.

50. Kun, *Bukharin*, 233–234.

51. Montefiore, *The Young Stalin*, 115–116.

52. Larina, *This I Cannot Forget*, 117.

53. Larina, *This I Cannot Forget*, 117.

54. Larina, *This I Cannot Forget*, 223.

55. The transcripts of this plenum, and accompanying notes and appendices, are found in Danilov, *Kak lomali NEP*, 2.

56. Danilov, *Kak lomali NEP*, 2:8.

57. Danilov, *Kak lomali NEP*, 2:6.

58. Danilov, *Kak lomali NEP*, 4:576.

59. Danilov, *Kak lomali NEP*, 4:538–539.

60. Danilov, *Kak lomali NEP*, 4:561.

61. Archives of the Soviet Communist Party, RGASPI (Russian State Archives of Social and Political History), f. 17, o. 2, d. 360, 61–88 (Hoover Institution Archives); Danilov, *Kak lomali NEP*, 2:180–206.

62. Danilov, *Kak lomali NEP*, 2:359.

63. Danilov, *Kak lomali NEP*, 2:360.

64. Danilov, *Kak lomali NEP*, 2:361.

65. Danilov, *Kak lomali NEP*, 2:364.

66. Danilov, *Kak lomali NEP*, 2:364.

67. Danilov, *Kak lomali NEP*, 2:376.

68. Archives, RGASPI, f. 17, o. 2, d. 367, 31–32, 59; d. 368, 32–34; Danilov, *Kak lomali NEP*, 2:379–381.

69. Aleksei Stetskii, head of propaganda for the northwest bureau of the Central Committee and former editor of *Komsomol'skaia Pravda*.

70. Archives, RGASPI, f. 17, o. 2, d. 367, 34–35; d. 368, 35–36; Danilov, *Kak lomali NEP*, 2:382.

71. Archives, RGASPI, f. 17, o. 2, d. 367, 74–76; Danilov, *Kak lomali NEP*, 2:391–397.

72. Danilov, *Kak lomali NEP*, 2:590–591.

73. Kun, *Bukharin*, 234.

74. Danilov, *Kak lomali NEP*, 2:573.

75. Larina, *This I Cannot Forget*, 114–115.

76. Robert Davies and Stephen Wheatcroft, *The Years of Hunger: Soviet Agriculture 1931–1933* (New York: MacMillan Palgrave, 2004), 431–440.

77. Larina, *This I Cannot Forget*, 127.

78. Larina, *This I Cannot Forget*, 115.

79. Larina, *This I Cannot Forget*, 115–116.

80. Larina, *This I Cannot Forget*, 115.

81. Larina, *This I Cannot Forget*, 117.

82. Bukharin letter to members of the Politburo and A. Ia. Vyshinsky, 27 August 1936, APRF (Archive of the President of the Russian Federation), f.3, d. 24, 67–82.

83. Danilov, *Kak lomali NEP*, 4:563.

84. Danilov, *Kak lomali NEP*, 4:559.

85. These letters and Bukharin's declaration are found in Danilov, *Kak lomali NEP*, 4: 564–567, 572–576.

86. Danilov, *Kak lomali NEP*, 4:576.

87. Danilov, *Kak lomali NEP*, 4:573–575.

88. Danilov, *Kak lomali NEP*, 4:573.

89. Miklós Kun, *Stalin: An Unknown Portrait* (Budapest: CEU Press, 2003), 291.

90. Allilueva, *Dvadtsat' pisem*, 29.

91. Hiroyaki Kuromiya, *Stalin: Profiles in Power* (Harlow, England: Pearson Longman, 2005), 42–43.

92. Kun, *Stalin*, 421; Kuromiya, *Stalin*, 59. The story is ascribed to Karl Radek, a close friend of Bukharin and a victim of Stalin.

93. Larina, *This I Cannot Forget*, 142, 323–324.

94. The story of Anna Larina's adoption and early years is told in Larina, *This I Cannot Forget*, 204–218.

95. This account of Larin's life is from *Bol'shaia Sovetskaia Entsiklopediia*, 3rd edition (Moscow: Sovetskaia Entsiklopediia, 1973), vol. 14, 487; Archives of L. O. Dan, *Memoirs of L. O. Dan* (Amsterdam: 1987), 3–130; and Aleksei Popov, *Iurii Larin, Sovetskikh kreativnykh idei*, 1k.com.ua/91/details/9/1. (accessed July 25, 2009).

96. Larina, *This I Cannot Forget*, 105, 204–219.

97. Larina, *This I Cannot Forget*, 281.

98. V. I. Lenin, "Polnoe sobranie sochinenii," vol. 45, 125 (cited in Larina, *This I Cannot Forget*, 215).

99. Larisa Vasil'eva, *Kremlin Wives* (New York: Arcade Publishing, 1992), 175.

100. Larina, *This I Cannot Forget*, 230.

101. Title of chapter from purported statement of Stalin as reported by Kamenev regarding his conversation with Bukharin, Danilov, *Kak lomali NEP*, 4:562–563.

102. This section is based on Danilov, *Kak lomali NEP*, 4: 577–601.

103. Danilov, *Kak lomali NEP*, 4:592.

104. Danilov, *Kak lomali NEP*, 4:588.

105. Danilov, *Kak lomali NEP*, 4:595.

106. Danilov, *Kak lomali NEP*, 4:95.

107. Danilov, *Kak lomali NEP*, 4:596–597.

108. Danilov, *Kak lomali NEP*, 4:597.

109. Danilov, *Kak lomali NEP*, 4: 540–548.

110. Kun, *Bukharin*, 252.

111. Larina, *This I Cannot Forget*, 124.

112. Larina, *This I Cannot Forget*, 124.

113. Danilov, *Kak lomali NEP*, 4:6.

114. Danilov, *Kak lomali NEP*, 4:12.

115. Danilov, *Kak lomali NEP*, 4:162.

116. Archives, RGASPI, f. 17, o. 2, d. 404, 86; Danilov, *Kak lomali NEP*, 4:162.

117. Archives, RGASPI, f. 17, o. 2, d. 404, 102; Danilov, *Kak lomali NEP*, 4:168.

118. Archives, RGASPI, f. 17, o. 2, d. 404, 105; d. 415; Danilov, *Kak lomali NEP*, 4:169.

119. Danilov, *Kak lomali NEP*, 4:172.

120. Archives, RGASPI, f. 17, o. 2, d. 404, 107; Danilov, *Kak lomali NEP*, 4:170.

121. Archives, RGASPI, f. 17, o. 2, d. 404, 70; Danilov, *Kak lomali NEP*, 4:154.

122. Danilov, *Kak lomali NEP*, 4:12.

123. Archives, RGASPI, f. 17, o. 2, d. 404, 144; Danilov, *Kak lomali NEP*, 4:184.

124. Archives, RGASPI, f. 17, o. 2, d. 404, 60, 88, 90; d. 415, 383; d. 416, 424; Danilov, *Kak lomali NEP*, 4:151, 163–164.

125. Archives, RGASPI, f. 17, o. 2, d. 404, 98 Danilov, *Kak lomali NEP*, 4:167.

126. Archives, RGASPI, f. 17, o. 2, d. 404, 158; Danilov, *Kak lomali NEP*, 4:190.

127. Archives, RGASPI, f. 17, o. 2, d. 404, 153; Danilov, *Kak lomali NEP*, 4:187; A. V. Kvashonkin et al., *Sovetskoe rukovodstvo, Perepiska, 1928–1941* (Moscow: Rosspen, 1999), 38–39.

128. Archives, RGASPI, f. 17, o. 2, d. 404, 154–156; d. 415, 120; Danilov, *Kak lomali NEP*, 4:188–189.

129. Archives, RGASPI, f. 17, o. 2, d. 417, 120; Danilov, *Kak lomali NEP*, 4:644.

130. Archives, RGASPI, f. 17, o. 2, d. 417, 120; Danilov, *Kak lomali NEP*, 4:645.

131. Archives, RGASPI, f. 17, o. 2, d. 417, 120; Danilov, *Kak lomali NEP*, 4:645–646.

132. Archives, RGASPI, f. 17, o. 2, d. 417, 121; Danilov, *Kak lomali NEP*, 4:647.

133. Archives, RGASPI, f. 17, o. 2, d. 417, 122; Danilov, *Kak lomali NEP*, 4:649.

134. Archives, RGASPI, f. 17, o. 2, d. 417, 124; Danilov, *Kak lomali NEP*, 4:654.

135. Archives, RGASPI, f. 17, o. 2, d. 416, 236; d. 417, 124; Danilov, *Kak lomali NEP*, 4:654.

136. Archives, RGASPI, f. 17, o. 2, d. 417, 125; Danilov, *Kak lomali NEP*, 4: 657–658.

137. Danilov, *Kak lomali NEP*, 4:659.

138. Danilov, *Kak lomali NEP*, 4:659–660.

139. Archives, RGASPI, f. 17, o. 2, d. 417, 131; Danilov, *Kak lomali NEP*, 4:673–674.

140. Archives, RGASPI, f. 17, o. 2, d. 417, 126–127; Danilov, *Kak lomali NEP*, 4:661–663.

141. Archives, RGASPI, f. 17, o. 2, d. 417, 127; Danilov, *Kak lomali NEP*, 4:663–664.

142. Archives, RGASPI, f. 17, o. 2, d. 417, 130; Danilov, *Kak lomali NEP*, 4:670–671.

143. Archives, RGASPI, f. 17, o. 2, d. 417, 132 ; Danilov, *Kak lomali NEP*, 4:676.

144. Archives, RGASPI, f. 17, o. 2, d. 417, 132; Danilov, *Kak lomali NEP,* 4:677.

145. Danilov, *Kak lomali NEP,* 4:682.

146. Danilov, *Kak lomali NEP,* 4:682.

147. Danilov, *Kak lomali NEP,* 4:683.

148. Danilov, *Kak lomali NEP,* 4:683–684.

149. Archives, RGASPI, f. 17, o. 2, d. 417, 134; Danilov, *Kak lomali NEP,* 4:684.

150. Kun, *Bukharin,* 285.

151. *Istochnik,* no. 3 (2000), 49.

152. V. N. Khaustov, V. P. Naumov, and N. S. Plotnikova, *Lubyanka: Stalin i glavnoe upravelnie gosbezopasnosti NKVD 1937–1938* (Moscow: Demokratiya, 2004), 32. Special communication from Ezhov to Stalin, January 11, 1937, on the interrogation of V. N. Astrov.

153. Larina, *This I Cannot Forget,* 140–142.

154. E. G. Oldenburg, "Iz dnevnikovykh zapisei (1925–1930)," *Vestnik Rossiiskoi Akademii nauk,* vol. 4, no. 7, 1994, 638–649.

155. Khaustov, *Lubyanka,* 234 (letter of I. I. Mezhlauk to V. M. Molotov about his deputy in the committee of the Higher School).

156. This section is based on Cohen, *Bukharin,* 332–336.

157. Kun, *Bukharin,* 292–293.

158. V. M. Zhukhrai, *Stalin: Pravda i lozh'* (Moscow: Svarog, 1996) (accessed November 28, 2009 from http://lib.thewalls.ru/zhukhrai/juhray01.htm).

159. Cohen, *Bukharin,* 334.

160. Quoted in Cohen, *Bukharin,* 335.

161. O. V. Khlevniuk et al., *Stalinskoe Politburo v 30-e gody* (Moscow: AIRO-xx, 1995), 94–95.

162. Danilov, *Kak lomali NEP,* 5: 10.

163. Archives, RGASPI, f. 17, op.162, d. 8, 64–69; "About Measures for the liquidation of kulak households in the regions of continuous collectivization," January 30, 1930. Appendix No. 2 to Protocol of the Politburo No. 116.

164. Oleg Khlevniuk, "Stalin, Syrtsov, Lominadze: Preparations for the 'Second Great Breakthrough,'" in Gregory and Naimark, eds., *The Lost Politburo Transcripts,* 78–96.

165. Larina, *This I Cannot Forget,* 127.

166. Roy Medvedev, *Nikolai Bukharin: The Last Years* (New York: W.W. Norton, 1980), 25; Kun, *Bukharin,* 297.

167. Kun, *Bukharin,* 310–312.

168. Kun, *Bukharin,* 312.

169. Larina, *This I Cannot Forget,* 107–112.

170. Kun, *Bukharin,* 304–305.

171. Bukharin's letter of October 14, 1930, is quoted in Khlevniuk, *Stalinskoe Politburo,* 38.

172. Kvashonkin et al., *Sovetskoe rukovodstvo, Perepiska, 1928–1941,* 146–147.

173. Larina, *This I Cannot Forget,* 136.

174. Larina, *This I Cannot Forget,* 229.

175. Larina, *This I Cannot Forget*, 143.

176. Larina, *This I Cannot Forget*, 146.

177. Vladimir Nekrasov, *Trinadtsat' zheleznykh narkomov: Istoriia NKVD-MVD ot A.I. Rykova do N.A. Shchelokova, 1917–1982* (Moscow: Versty, 1995), 175.

178. O. V. Khlevniuk, R. Davies, L. P. Kosheleva, E. A. Ris, L. A. Rogovaia, *Stalin i Kaganovich. Perepiski. 1931–1936 gg.* (Moscow: Rosspen, 2001), 683.

179. These transcripts are from art-bin.com/art/omosc23m.html, http://art-bin .com/art/amosc_preeng.html (accessed November 19, 2009).

180. Kun, *Bukharin*, 50–52.

181. Larina, *This I Cannot Forget*, 139.

182. Archives, RGASPI, f. 558, o. 11, d. 710, 172–178.

183. Larina, *This I Cannot Forget*, 248.

184. Larina, *This I Cannot Forget*, 64.

185. Kun, *Stalin*, 235.

186. Archives, RGANI (Russian State Archive of Contemporary History), f. 6, o. 1, d. 49, 106–122.

187. Larina, *This I Cannot Forget*, 254.

188. Cohen, *Bukharin*, 365–366.

189. Andrè Liebich, "I Am the Last—Memories of Bukharin in Paris," *Slavic Review*, vol. 51, no. 4 (Winter 1992), 767–781.

190. Cohen, *Bukharin*, 472.

191. The account of Bukharin's trip to Uzbekistan is found in Larina, *This I Cannot Forget*, 86.

192. "Poslednie pis'ma N. I. Bukharina I. V. Stalinu," *Istorichesky arkhiv*, no. 3 (2001), 67–68.

193. APRF, f. 3, o. 24, d. 235, 118–120

194. Larina, *This I Cannot Forget*, 289.

195. Letter from Bukharin to members of the Politburo and A. Ia. Vyshinsky, August 27, 1936, APRF, f. 3, d. 235, 67–82.

196. "N. I. Bukharin Letter to Stalin, I. V., November 16, 1936," *Istorichesky arkhiv*, no. 3 (2001), 72–73.

197. Nikita Petrov, *Pervyi predsedatel' KGB Ivan Serov* (Moscow: Materik, 2005), 313–315.

198. Archives, RGASPI, f. 17, o. 2, d. 574, 7.

199. Archives, RGASPI, f. 17, o. 2, d. 574, 49.

200. Archives, RGASPI, f. 17, o. 2, d. 574, 50.

201. Archives, RGASPI, f. 17, o. 2, d. 574, 2–3.

202. Former head of the Moscow party organization, a colleague of Bukharin. He was executed in 1937.

203. Former regional party secretary and deputy director of Lenin library. Sentenced to the Gulag, he died there.

204. Archives, RGASPI, f. 17, o. 2, d. 574, 4–6.

205. Archives, RGASPI, f. 17, o. 2, d. 574, 3.

206. Archives, RGASPI, f. 17, o. 2, d. 574, 8.

207. Archives, RGASPI, f. 17, o. 2, d. 573, 30–33.

208. Archives, RGASPI, f. 17, o. 2, d. 574, 17.

209. Archives, RGASPI, f. 17, o. 2, d. 574, 39–44.

210. Archives, RGASPI, f. 17, o. 2, d. 574, 97.
211. Larina, *This I Cannot Forget*, 301.
212. Archives, RGASPI, f. 17, o. 2, d. 574, 70.
213. Larina, *This I Cannot Forget*, 324.
214. Larina, *This I Cannot Forget*, 304.
215. Larina, *This I Cannot Forget*, 304.
216. Archives, RGASPI, f. 17, o. 2, d. 574, 26.
217. "Confrontation of N. I. Bukharin with Karl Radek, January 13, 1937," *Istochnik*, no. 1 (2001), 63–77.
218. Petrov, *Pervyi predsedatel'*, 313–315.
219. Larina, *This I Cannot Forget*, 312.
220. Larina, *This I Cannot Forget*, 312.
221. "Politicheskii arkhiv XX veka. Materialy fevral'sko-martovoskogo plenuma TsK VKP (b) 1937 goda," *Voprosy istorii*, no. 2 (1992), 5–6. For Larina's version, see Larina, *This I Cannot Forget*, 323. In this discussion of the February–March plenum, I use both the "corrected" versions published in *Voprosy istorii* in 1992 and the "uncorrected" version from Archives, RGASPI, f. 17, o. 2, d. 579, 581, 583.
222. Larina, *This I Cannot Forget*, 329–330.
223. Larina, *This I Cannot Forget*, 331.
224. Archives, RGASPI, f. 17, o. 2, d. 579, 1a–59. For the "corrected" transcript of the plenum, see "Politicheskii arkhiv XX veka. Materialy fevral'sko-martovskogo plenuma TsK VKP (b) 1937 goda," *Voprosy istorii*, no. 2 (1992), 3–34; no. 4 (1992), 3–36; no. 6 (1992), 3–39.
225. *Voprosy istorii*, no. 4 (1992), 16–17; Archives, RGASPI, f. 17, o. 2, d. 579, 63–68.
226. Bukharin's remarks are from *Voprosy istorii*, no. 4 (1992), 24–36; Archives, RGASPI, f. 17, o. 2, d. 579, 99–101.
227. Larina, *This I Cannot Forget*, 331–332.
228. Bukharin's February 24 evening statement is from *Voprosy istorii*, no. 6 (1992), 2–3; Archives, RGASPI, f. 17, o. 2, d. 581, 2–3.
229. Archives, RGASPI, f. 17, o. 2, d. 583, 109–110.
230. Archives, RGASPI, f. 17, o. 2, d. 582, 7.
231. Larina, *This I Cannot Forget*, 333.
232. Larina, *This I Cannot Forget*, 345.
233. *Voprosy istorii*, no. 4 (1992), 3–16; Archives, RGASPI, f. 17, o. 2, d. 579, 1a–59.
234. *Voprosy istorii*, no. 4 (1992), 10; Archives, RGASPI, f. 17, o. 2, d. 579, 33.
235. *Voprosy istorii*, no. 4 (1992), 4; Archives, RGASPI, f. 17, o. 2, d. 579, 3.
236. *Voprosy istorii*, no. 4 (1992), 16; Archives, RGASPI, f. 17, o. 2, d. 579, 59.
237. *Stenogramma ochnoi stavki v TsK VKP(b) mezhdu Bukharinym N. I. i Kulikovym ot 7 dekabria 1936 goda*, APRF, f 3, o. 24, d. 260, 84–116.
238. *Voprosy istorii*, no. 4 (1992), 21; Archives, RGASPI, f. 17, o. 2, d. 579, 86.
239. *Voprosy istorii*, no. 4 (1992), 22; Archives, RGASPI, f. 17, o. 2, d. 579, hives90
240. *Voprosy istorii*, no. 4 (1992), 24; Archives, RGASPI, f. 17, o. 2, d. 579, 98, 103.
241. *Voprosy istorii*, no. 4 (1992), 25; Archives, RGASPI, f. 17, o. 2, d. 579, 104.

242. *Voprosy istorii*, no. 4 (1992), 31; Archives, RGASPI, f. 17, o. 2, d. 579, 132.

243. *Voprosy istorii*, no. 4 (1992), 26; Archives, RGASPI, f. 17, o. 2, d. 579, 108.

244. *Voprosy istorii*, no. 4 (1992), 26; Archives, RGASPI, f. 17, o. 2, d. 579, 109.

245. *Voprosy istorii*, no. 4 (1992), 26–27; Archives, RGASPI, f. 17, o. 2, d. 579, 110–112.

246. *Voprosy istorii*, no. 4 (1992), 27; Archives, RGASPI, f. 17, o. 2, d. 579, 112.

247. *Voprosy istorii*, no. 4 (1992), 28; Archives, RGASPI, f. 17, o. 2, d. 579, 115–116.

248. *Voprosy istorii*, no. 4 (1992), 28; Archives, RGASPI, f. 17, o. 2, d. 579, 117–118.

249. *Voprosy istorii*, no. 4 (1992), 31–33; Archives, RGASPI, f. 17, o. 2, d. 579, 136–151.

250. Their speeches are in Archives, RGASPI, f. 17, o. 2, d. 582.

251. Larina, *This I Cannot Forget*, 332–323.

252. Archives, RGASPI, f. 17, o. 2, d. 577, 25–31.

253. Bukharin's arrest warrant is in Dmitrii A. Volkogonov, A Registry of his Papers, Library of Congress, Box 3, Folder 55 (Papka No. 55).

254. Larina, *This I Cannot Forget*, 335–336.

255. Larina, *This I Cannot Forget*, 201–202, 316–317.

256. A. V. Kvashonkin et al., *Sovetskoe rukovodstvo, Perepiska, 1928–1941* (Moscow: Rosspen, 1999). Bukharin's letter to Stalin of December 10, 1937.

257. Nikolai Bukharin (translated by George Shriver), *How It All Began* (New York: Columbia University Press, 1999); Nikolai Bukharin, *Philosophical Arabesques* (New York: Monthly Review Press, 2005). See also: Ronald Grigor Suny, "The Prison Notebooks," *Nation*, August 28, 2006.

258. Bukharin's "personal confession" is in Volkogonov, A Registry, Library of Congress, Box 3, Folder 5 (Papka No. 55). An English translation can be found in Grover Ferr and Valdimir Bobrov, *Pervye priznatel'nye pokazaniia N. I. Bukharina na Lubianke* www.delostalina.ru/?p=17 (Accessed November 19, 2009).

259. Ferr and Bobrov, *Pervye priznatel'nye pokazaniia*; and www.delostalina.ru/?p=17.

260. A. Artizov et al., *Reabilitatsiia: Kak eto bylo* (Moscow: Demokratiia, 2004), 48.

261. Kun, *Bukharin*, 388.

262. Larina, *This I Cannot Forget*, 60–61.

263. Andrey Vyshinsky's summation in English translation is in *Soviet Russia Today*, April 1938, vol. 7, no. 2.

264. Il'ia Erenburg, *Liudi, gody, zhizn'*, vol. 2 (Moscow: Tekst, 2005), 202.

265. These transcripts are from art-bin.com/art/omosc23m.html and artbin.com/art/amosc_preeng.html.

266. Larina, *This I Cannot Forget*, 67.

267. "V Prezidium Verkhovnogo Soveta SSSR, prigovorennogo k rasstrelu N. Bukharina, Proshchenie," GARF f.7523, o. 66, de. 58, 1–4.

268. Jacob Heilbrunn, "*The New York Times* and the Moscow Show Trials," *World Affairs*, vol. 153, no. 3 (Winter 1991), 92–93.

269. Harold Denny, "Soviet Aide Asserts Guilt, Again Reversing Himself," *New York Times*, Microfiche Archive, March 4, 1938.

270. Joseph Davies, *Mission to Moscow* (New York: Simon and Schuster, 1941), 269–70.

271. PA AA, B Moskau, Bd. 107 (Political Archive of the German Federal Foreign Office, Embassy in Moscow, vol. 107).

272. Redman, Joseph, "The British Stalinists and the Moscow Trials," *Labour Review*, vol. 3, no. 2 (March–April 1958), 44–53.

273. Corliss Lamont et al., "An Open Letter to American Liberals," *Soviet Russia Today* (March 1937).

274. "Moe poslednee slovo na sude, veroiatno, budet moim poslednimm slovom voobsche," Kto i kak pravil rech' N. I. Bukharina, *Istochnik*, no. 4 (1996), 78–92.

275. Report of Court Proceedings in the Case of the Anti-Soviet "Bloc of Rights and Trotskyites," March 2–13, 1938 (Moscow: People's Commissariat of Justice, 1938).

276. Cohen, *Bukharin*, 380–381.

277. Iurii Murin, *Istoriia odnogo priznaniia*, sovsekretno.ru/magazines/article/1979.

278. This letter is an edited extract from Getty, *The Road to Terror*, 559.

279. Murin, *Istoriia*, sovsekretno.ru/magazines/article/1979.

280. Kun, *Bukharin*, 466.

281. Larina, *This I Cannot Forget*, 85–90.

282. Larina, *This I Cannot Forget*, 162–163.

283. Larina, *This I Cannot Forget*, 186.

284. *Istochnik*, no. 2 (2001), 89

285. *Istochnik*, no. 2 (2001), 90.

286. Larina, *This I Cannot Forget*, 203.

287. Larina, *This I Cannot Forget*, 203.

288. Larina, *This I Cannot Forget*, 319–322.

289. "Widow of the Revolution: The Anna Larina Story," documentary film, 2000.

290. "Widow of the Revolution."

291. Artizov, *Reabilitatsiia*, 48.

292. The story of Bukharin's rehabilitation is told by Stephen Cohen on pages 23–29 of his introduction to Larina's autobiography, *This I Cannot Forget*.

293. Marc Junge, *Bucharin's Rehabilitierung: Historisches Gedaechtnis in der Sowjetunion 1953–1992* (Bochum: BasisDruck, 1999), 300–310, 312–314.

294. Cohen, *Bukharin*.

295. Vadimir Terebilov, member of Central Committee, born 1916.

296. Anatolii Luk'ianov, candidate member, Politburo, born 1930.

297. Aleksandr Rekunkov, member of Central Committee, born 1920.

298. Mikhail Solomentsev, member of Politburo, born 1913.

299. Larina, *This I Cannot Forget*, 356.

300. Two books that focus on the experiences of primarily ordinary people in the course of Stalin's purges are Hiroiaki Kuromiya, *Voices of the Dead: Stalin's Great Terror in the 1930s* (New Haven: Yale University Press, 2007); and Orlando Figes, *The Whisperers: Private Lives in Stalin's Russia* (New York: Metropolitan Books, 2007).

301. Cohen, *Bukharin*, 286–291.

302. Kun, *Bukharin*, 233–234.

303. Carr, "The Legend of Bukharin," 1.

304. F. A. Hayek, *The Road to Serfdom* (Chicago: University of Chicago Press, 1944).

305. Stephen Cohen, *Soviet Fates and Lost Alternatives: From Stalinism to the Cold War* (New York: Columbia University Press, 2009), chap. 1.

306. Cohen, *Soviet Fates*, 25.

307. Gregory, *Terror by Quota*, 106–139.

308. F. I. Chev, *Sto sorok besed s Molotovym* (Moscow: Terra, 1991); F. I. Chuev, *Tak Govoril Kaganovich* (Moscow: Otchestvo, 1991).

309. Nikolai Baibakov, *Ot Stalina do El'tsina* (Moscow: Gazoil Press, 1998), 11.

310. "Ni razu ne govorilos' otnositel'no terrora," Stenograma ochnoi stavki N. I. Bukharina s N. V. Astrovym v Politburo TsK VKP(b) 13 ianvaria 1937," *Istochnik*, no. 1 (2001), 94.

311. Arthur Koestler, *Darkness at Noon* (New York: MacMillan, 1941).

312. Cohen, *Bukharin and the Bolshevik Revolution*, 337–381.

313. Nikolai Bukharin, *Vremena: Roman* (Moskva: Izdatel'skaia gruppa "Progress," "Kul'tura," 1994), 130.

Cast of Characters

ALLILUEVA, NADEZHDA (Nadya) (1901–32). Stalin's second wife, friend of Bukharin, married Stalin in 1918, son Vasilii (1921–62) and daughter Svetlana (born in 1926), committed suicide in November 1932.

ALLILUEVA, SVETLANA (b. 1926). Stalin's only daughter, childhood friend of Bukharin's daughter (also named Svetlana), graduated from Moscow State University, several dissolved marriages, emigrated in 1967, naturalized U.S. citizen and author, lives in Madison, Wisconsin.

ASTROV, VALENTIN (1898–1993). Journalist-writer, on editorial board of *Pravda* and member of the Bukharin faction in the Institute of Red Professors, removed from his positions in 1928, arrested in 1933, gave testimony against Bukharin and was imprisoned, freed in 1937 by order of Stalin, one of the few survivors of the Bukharin school.

BERIIA, LAVRENTII (1899–1953). In 1926 became the head of the Georgian NKVD, in 1932 became Trans-Caucasian party head, in November 1938 replaced Ezhov as head of the NKVD, in 1934 became member of the Central Committee, went on to become deputy of the USSR, prime minister, head of the Ministry of Internal Affairs, and member of the Politburo from 1946 to 1953, executed in December.

BUDENNYI, SEMEN (1883–1973). Commander of the First Red Army Cavalry during the civil war, marshal of the Soviet Union (1935), head of the Moscow Military District during the 1937 military purges, a close associate of Stalin's, and member of the Central Committee (1939–52).

BUKHARIN, IVAN (1860–1940). Father of Bukharin, retired math teacher.

BUKHARIN, NIKOLAI (1888–1938). Also referred to as Nikolai Ivanovich; nicknames: Bukharka, Bukhashka.

BUKHARIN (GUSMAN, LARIN), IURA (b. 1936). Son of Nikolai Bukharin and Anna Larina, raised in orphanages and foster homes, reunited with his mother in 1956, now an artist living in Moscow.

DAN, FEDOR (1871–1947). Menshevik leader exiled in 1922, Bukharin's counterpart in the negotiations to purchase the Marx archive in Paris in 1936, died in New York.

DZERZHINSKII, FELIKS (1877–1926). Polish communist leader in prerevolutionary period, first head of the secret police (the Cheka/OGPU) (1917–26), commissar of transport, head of the Supreme Council of National Economy, candidate member of the Politburo, died of a heart attack.

ENUKIDZE, AVEL' (1877–1937). Georgian, childhood friend of Stalin's, Svetlana Allilueva's godfather, placed in charge of Kremlin security, member of the Central Committee (1934–35), and executed on Stalin's orders as a leader of an alleged plot to overthrow Stalin.

ERENBURG, IL'IA (1891–1967). Author and correspondent, high school friend of Bukharin's, one of USSR's most famous authors, he tested the limits of censorship, was an eyewitness to the Bukharin trial, and received three Stalin Prizes.

EZHOV, NIKOLAI (1895–1940). Minor party official who rose to power based on his personal loyalty to Stalin, replaced Iagoda as head of the NKVD in 1936, in charge of investigating Bukharin, conducted the Great Terror for Stalin, and was executed.

FRINOVSKII, MIKHAIL (1898–1940). Deputy head of the NKVD under Ezhov, then served as a government official and commissar of the navy before being executed.

FRUMKIN, MOISEI (1878–1938). Old Bolshevik, trade official and regional party official in Siberia and the Northern Caucasus, author of letter protesting Stalin's agrarian policies in 1928, later executed.

FRUNZE, MIKHAIL (1885–1925). Civil war hero, voted onto the Central Committee in 1921, candidate member of the Politburo in 1924, deputy commissar for military affairs in 1924, chairman of the Revolutionary Military Council in 1925, died of chloroform poisoning in an operation arranged by Stalin.

GORKY, MAKSIM (1868–1936). Russian/Soviet writer, founder of the genre of socialist realism, wrote favorably of Stalin but became disenchanted, died under mysterious circumstances.

GURVICH, ESFIR' (1895–1989). Bukharin's second wife (1920–29), trained as an architect and economist, an intimate of Nadezhda Allilueva's, divorced Bukharin in 1929, rightly fearful of her and their daughter's safety, they were both arrested and imprisoned in 1949.

GURVICH, SVETLANA (b. 1924). Daughter of Nikolai Bukharin and Esfir' Gurvich, playmate of Stalin's daughter, studied history at Moscow State University, arrested and imprisoned in 1949, lives in Moscow.

IAGODA, GENRIKH (1891–1938). Member of secret police beginning in 1920, deputy chairman of OGPU, first head of the NKVD on its founding in 1934, fired in 1936, before that responsible for carrying out Stalin's dekulakization campaign, executed along with Bukharin.

KAGANOVICH, LAZAR (1893–1991). Party secretary of Ukraine (1925–28) and then Moscow, member of the Politburo beginning in 1930, deputy of Stalin known for his cruelty, commissar of transport, commissar of heavy industry, commissar of oil industry, expelled from the party in 1961, died at the age of 97, defending Stalin to the end.

KALININ, MIKHAIL (1875–1946). Bolshevik revolutionary, member of Politburo and nominal head of the Soviet state from 1919 to 1946; although considered moderate, supported Stalin consistently.

KAMENEV (ROZENFEL'D), LEV (1883–1936). Old Bolshevik, Lenin's deputy in exile and during Lenin's administration, head of the Moscow Soviet (1918–25), member of the Politburo beginning in 1919, expelled from the party in 1926, meeting with Bukharin in July 1928 became the genesis of the so-called Left-Right bloc, executed as a defendant in the first Moscow Show Trial after testifying against Bukharin, youngest son, Iurii, died in prison in 1938, son Aleksandr was executed in 1939, wife Olga, Trotsky's sister, executed in 1941.

KIROV, SERGEI (1886–1934). Party member beginning in 1904, commander of the Bolshevik military administration in Astrakhan, party secretary of Azerbaizhan (1921), party secretary of Leningrad starting in 1926, member of the Politburo (1930), won most votes for reelection to the Central Committee in the party congress of 1934, assassination in December gave Stalin a reason to purge the party leadership.

KRESTINSKII, NIKOLAI (1883–1938). Old Bolshevik, member of the first Politburo, secretary of the Central Committee, commissar of finance (1918–22), Trotsky supporter until 1927, lost party posts, ambassador to Germany (1921), deputy foreign minister (1930–37), worked as a diplomat until his arrest in 1937, sole defendant at the third Moscow Show Trial to plead innocent, executed along with Bukharin.

KRUPSKAYA, NADEZHDA (1869–1939). Russian Bolshevik revolutionary, married Lenin in 1888, exiled with him in Siberia and Europe, deputy commissar of education (1917), member of Central Committee, friend of Bukharin's, opponent of Stalin's in 1926, later tried to remain above party politics, died of food poisoning.

KULIKOV, EGOR (1891–1943). Party member beginning in 1910, secretary of a regional committee party in Moscow province (1925–28), member of the Central Committee (1925–1930), Bukharin, Rykov, and Tomskii loyalist, labeled as a "rightist" and arrested in 1935, accused Bukharin of ordering Stalin's assassination, died in prison.

LARIN (born Lurie), **IURII** (1880–1932). Stepfather of Anna Larina, close friend of Bukharin's, revolutionary leader in Petrograd, appointed by Lenin to numerous state committees.

LARINA, ANNA ("Larochka," "Annushka"), (1914–96).

LARINA, LENA (1891–?). Stepmother of Anna Larina, her deceased mother's sister, sentenced to eight years in prison in April 1938, released in February 1946, in

February 1950 sentenced to penal colony in Kazakhstan, sentenced to five years in a prison labor camp in July 1957.

LENIN (Ul'ianov), **VLADIMIR** ("Il'ich") (1870–1924). Leader of the Bolshevik Party, in 1903 split off the Bolsheviks from the Mensheviks, arrested and exiled, returned to Russia to participate in the 1905–7 Russian revolution, exiled again in 1907, returned to Russia by the Germans during the 1917 revolution, headed the first Soviet government, ordered Red Terror, incapacitated by strokes beginning in May 1922, died without naming a successor, embalmed body exhibited in the Lenin Mausoleum on Red Square.

LITVINOV, MAKSIM (1876–1951). Born to a poor Jewish family in Russian Poland, party member from 1898, Bolshevik from 1903, experienced diplomat, deputy commissar of foreign affairs (1921), commissar of foreign affairs (1930), replaced by Molotov shortly before the nonaggression pact with Hitler, member of the Central Committee (1934–41), ambassador to the United States (1941–43) and Cuba (1942–43), retired in 1946, died in a suspicious car accident in Moscow.

LUKINA-BUKHARINA, NADEZHDA (1887–1940). Bukharin's first cousin, married Bukharin in 1911, separated in 1920, active Russian revolutionary, Bolshevik Party member, an editor of the *Small Soviet Encyclopedia,* after becoming bedridden lived in the Bukharins' Kremlin apartment after the marriage of Bukharin and Anna Larina, resigned from the party, arrested April 30, 1938, and then executed.

LUNACHARSKY, ANATOLY (1875–1933). Russian Marxist revolutionary, writer, journalist, and philosopher, first commissar of education (1917–29), USSR representative at the League of Nations (1930), died in France en route to Spain to become its ambassador.

MAYAKOVSKY, VLADIMIR (1893–1930). Marxist revolutionary activist, renowned Russian and Soviet poet, playwright, critic, and graphic designer, a founder of the Russian Futurism movement in poetry, allowed to travel freely in the West in the 1920s, committed suicide.

MEKHLIS, LEV (1889–1953). Party member beginning in 1918, Stalin loyalist and editor of *Pravda* from 1930 to 1937, frequent critic of Bukharin, political commissar of the Red Army (1937–42).

MIKOIAN, ANASTAS (1895–1978). Party member beginning in 1915, Stalin loyalist, longtime head of trade ministry, member of the Central Committee (1923), full member of Politburo (1935), head of the government under Khrushchev and Brezhnev (1964–65), retired in 1965.

MOLOTOV, VYACHESLAV (1890–1986). Stalin loyalist, Politburo member, head of the government (1930–41) and foreign affairs (1939–49, 1953–56), expelled from the Politburo in June 1957, removed from all positions and expelled from the party (1961), retired in March 1962, restored his membership in the party in 1984, died at the age of 96 in Moscow.

NICOLAEVSKY, BORIS (1887–1966). Russian Marxist revolutionary, Bolshevik (1903–6), then Menshevik (1906), émigré historian (1922), representative abroad of the Moscow Marx and Engels Institute (1924–31), negotiator with Bukharin for the purchase of the Marx archive in Paris (1936), noted collector of Russian political documents, which he contributed to the Hoover Institution at Stanford, California, died in New York City.

ORDZHONIKIDZE, GRIGORII ("Comrade Sergo") (1886–1937). Georgian party leader, brought to Moscow as a Stalin loyalist, member of the Central Committee and Politburo member (1926), chair of the Supreme Economic Council of the USSR (1930–33), commissar of heavy industry (1932–37), died of an apparent suicide.

PIATAKOV, GEORGII (Iurii) (1890–1937). Party member beginning in 1910, Trotsky supporter after Lenin's death, member of the Central Committee (1923–27, 1930–36), deputy commissar of heavy industry (1931–32), arrested in September 1936, executed as a defendant in the second Moscow Show Trial.

RADEK, KARL (1885–1939). Worked with Lenin in exile, member of the Central Committee (1919–24), occupied high positions in the Comintern (1920–24), supporter of Leon Trotsky, expelled from the party and exiled in 1927, readmitted in 1930, served under Bukharin as a correspondent for *Izvestiia*, expelled from the party in 1936, sentenced to prison in the second Moscow Show Trial, killed in prison on orders of the NKVD.

RIUTIN, MARTEM'IAN (1890–1937). Old Bolshevik, official in Moscow City party organization, associate of Bukharin's, purported author of a political platform calling for Stalin's replacement, expelled from the party, arrested, sentenced to prison, and executed.

RYKOV, ALEKSEI (1881–1938). Old Bolshevik, member of the Central Committee beginning in 1920, member of Politburo, head of government after Lenin's death (1924–29), a leader along with Bukharin and Tomskii of the "right deviation," executed along with Bukharin.

SOKOL'NIKOV, GRIGORII (1888–1939). Childhood friend of Bukharin's, Old Bolshevik, member of the Central Committee (1917–19, 1922–30), signed the Brest-Litovsk Treaty in 1918, commander of the Turkestan front (1920–21), commissar of finance (1922–26), ambassador to Britain (1929–32), then served in the Foreign Office, sentenced to prison in the second Moscow Show Trial, killed by order of the NKVD in prison.

STALIN (Dzhugasvhvili), **IOSIF** (Joseph) (1878–1953). Preferred nickname Koba, disliked nickname Soso.

TOMSKII, MIKHAIL (1880–1936). Old Bolshevik, member of the Central Committee (1919–34) and Politburo (1922–30), head of Russian trade unions (1918–29), leader of the "right deviation" opposition to Stalin along with Bukharin and Rykov, committed suicide.

TRAVINA, ALEKSANDRA (Sasha). Assigned to be Bukharin's mistress and a secret informer, lived openly with Bukharin in 1930 and 1931, expelled from the party, fate undocumented.

TROTSKY, LEON (1879–1940). Commissar for foreign affairs (1917–18), commissar of war (1918–25), founder and commander of the Red Army during the civil war, joined with Kamenev and Zinovyev in the United Opposition (1926–27), expelled from the Politburo (1926) and the party (1927), exiled to Alma-Ata in 1927, deported to Turkey in February 1929, assassinated by an NKVD secret agent in Mexico, his sister Olga and his son Sergei were executed, his son Leon was poisoned.

TUKHACHEVSKII, MIKHAIL (1893–1937). Party member beginning in 1918, civil war hero in Siberia and Crimea, headed Red Army (1925–28), deputy commissar for defense (1931–37), marshal of the Soviet Union (1935), executed after a secret trial of military leaders.

UGLANOV, NIKOLAI (1886–1937). Bukharin ally, member of the Central Committee (1923–30), headed Moscow party committee (1924–28), expelled from the party in 1932, restored to membership (1934–36), shortly afterward executed.

UL'IANOVA, MARIIA (1878–1937). Lenin's sister, party member beginning in 1898, member of the editorial board and executive secretary of *Pravda* (1917–29), friend of Bukharin's, occupied many government positions, including working at the Lenin Institute beginning in 1929.

UL'RIKH, VASILII (1889–1951). Bolshevik (1910), secret police official beginning in 1918, head of the Military Collegium of the Soviet Supreme Court (1926–48), deputy chairman the Soviet Supreme Court (1935–38), presided at the Moscow Show Trials.

VOROSHILOV, KLIMENT (1881–1969). Old Bolshevik (1903), military leader, Stalin crony, member of the Central Committee (1921–1961), member of the Politburo (1926–60), people's commissar for military and navy affairs (1925), chairman of the Revolutionary Military Council until 1934, commissar of defense (1934–40), member of the State Defense Committee during World War II, head of Soviet state (1953–60).

VYSHINSKY, ANDREY (1883–1954). Menshevik (1903), Bolshevik (1920), academic lawyer and rector at Moscow University (1921–28), justice official beginning in 1923, chief procurator of the Russian Soviet Federated Socialist Republic (1931), chief procurator of the USSR (1935–39), prosecutor at Moscow Show Trials, foreign minister (1949–53), USSR's representative at the United Nations.

ZINOVYEV, GRIGORY (1883–1936). Bolshevik revolutionary figure, deputy of Lenin in exile, head of Petrograd/Leningrad Soviet (1917–26), member of Politburo (1917, 1921–26), head of the Comintern Executive Committee (1919–26), member of the United Opposition with Trotsky and Kamenev, expelled and exiled, arrested in December 1934, sentenced to ten years in prison, executed in the first Moscow Show Trial.

About the Author

Paul R. Gregory, a Hoover Institution research fellow, holds the Cullen Endowed Professorship in the Department of Economics at the University of Houston, Texas, and is a research professor at the German Institute for Economic Research in Berlin. He is also the chair of the International Advisory Board of the Kiev School of Economics. Gregory is the author of *Terror by Quota* (2009), *Lenin's Brain and Other Tales from the Secret Soviet Archives* (2008), and *The Political Economy of Stalinism* (2004), all based on his work in the Hoover Institution Archives. He has also coedited archival publications, such as the prize-winning seven-volume *History of Stalin's Gulag* (2004) and the three-volume *Stenograms of Meetings of the Politburo of the Central Committee* (2007). His publications have been awarded the Hewett Book Prize and the J.M. Montias Prize. Gregory is the coeditor of the Yale-Hoover series on Stalin, Stalinism, and Cold War. He divides his time between Houston, Palo Alto, and Berlin.

Index